Living Faithfully
in the
Time of Creation

We wish to thank the members of the Iona Community Common Concern Network on the Environment for their support for this book, especially our Moderator, Ran Nisbett, for his unfailing encouragement. We thank our global contributors for sharing their experience and wisdom. Special thanks to Neil Paynter and Sandra Kramer, editors extraordinaire, for their commitment to its publication in a short time-scale and under difficult circumstances.

Living Faithfully
in the
Time of Creation

Kathy Galloway & Katharine M. Preston (Eds)

wild goose
publications  www.**ionabooks**.com

First published 2021 by
Wild Goose Publications
Suite 9, Fairfield
1048 Govan Road, Glasgow G51 4XS, Scotland
the publishing division of the Iona Community.
Scottish Charity No. SC003794. Limited Company Reg. No. SC096243.

ISBN 978-1-84952-801-6

Cover image © David Coleman

The publishers gratefully acknowledge the support of the Drummond Trust,
3 Pitt Terrace, Stirling FK8 2EY in producing this book.

Overseas distribution
Australia: Willow Connection Pty Ltd, Unit 4A, 3–9 Kenneth Road,
Manly Vale, NSW 2093
New Zealand: Pleroma, Higginson Street, Otane 4170, Central Hawkes Bay

Printed by Bell & Bain, Thornliebank, Glasgow

Contents

Foreword, by Ruth Harvey   11

Introduction, by Kathy Galloway and Katharine M. Preston   13

Lectionary reflections   15

Introduction, by Kathy Galloway   16

15th Sunday after Pentecost (B), Liz Gibson   17

16th Sunday after Pentecost (B), Urzula Glienecke   20

17th Sunday after Pentecost (B), Stuart Elliott   24

18th Sunday after Pentecost (B), David Osborne   27

19th Sunday after Pentecost (B), Graham McGeoch   30

20th Sunday after Pentecost (B), Chris Polhill   33

21st Sunday after Pentecost (B), John McCulloch   36

22nd Sunday after Pentecost (B), Kathy Galloway   39

23rd Sunday after Pentecost (B), Liz Johnson Blythe   43

24th Sunday after Pentecost (B), Sally Foster-Fulton   46

25th Sunday after Pentecost (B), Tim Gorringe   49

Last Sunday of the Year: Reign of Christ (B), David J.M. Coleman   52

Sources and acknowledgements   56

Essays   57

Introduction, Katharine M. Preston   58

Drookit!, Val Brown   59

Just food for all, Elizabeth Dowler   61

Pilgrimage2Paris, Diana Hill   63

God made the earth … then man happened,
    Marksen Masinde and Fridah Wafula   66

Living lightly at Camas, Rachel McCann   68

Rising through the third great flood, Alastair McIntosh   71

Dicing with tipping points, Mike Mineter   73

Making a difference, Monica Mueller-Roemer   75

The climate crisis and biodiversity loss:
    Humility and healing on the twofold way, Richard A. Nisbett   77

Close to home, Katharine M. Preston   80

Love and rage, Eve Sharples   82

'The black summer', Helen Weavers   84

**God's Good Earth: A Service of Worship in Preparation for the COP26
Climate Change Conference, the Wild Goose Resource Group   87**

Introduction   88

Order of worship   90

Appendix   97

This is God's world, John L. Bell   97

On the eighth day, the Wild Goose Resource Group   98

Sources and acknowledgements   104

Liturgical resources   105

Calls to worship/opening responses and prayers   106

Gathering responses, Stuart Elliot   106

Call to worship, Kathy Galloway   106

Strengthen us, Mother God, Chris Polhill   107

Prayers of approach   107

A Celtic rune of hospitality   107

God of all life, Kathy Galloway   108

Confession/repentance/absolution   109

Free us for action, John Polhill   109

We did not know, Kathy Galloway   110

Meditations 111

If we had but a glimpse, Stuart Elliot 111
Wow!, Chris Polhill 111
The Wow of creation, David Hawkey 112
A lamentation and prayer of contrition to the whole of creation,
Richard A. Nisbett 114

Prayers/litanies of thanksgiving 118

Generous God, Kathy Galloway 118
Thank you for ordinary wonderful things, Richard Sharples 119
Prayer, John L. Bell 120
Rainbow litany, Kathy Galloway 121

Prayers of intercession and concern 122

God of all creation, Kathy Galloway 122
Together we stand strong, Kathy Galloway 123

Communion of saints 125

A prayer from Iona Abbey, Neil Paynter 125

Prayers of self-offering/commitment 126

A new heaven and a new earth, John Harrison 126

Prayers to go/blessing/benedictions 127

A Gaelic blessing 127
Blessing, Kathy Galloway 127
Blessing 127
Blessing, from the *Carmina Gadelica* 128

Additional resources 128

Sources and acknowledgements   129

Hymns and songs   131

Introduction, Kathy Galloway   132
God, in creating, bore and blessed, John L. Bell   133
The life of the world, Kathy Galloway   135
All the wonder that surrounds us, John L. Bell and Graham Maule   136
The sorrow, John L. Bell and Graham Maule   137
We will not take what is not ours, John L. Bell and Graham Maule   138
I will sing a song of love, John L. Bell   139
Monarch and maker of all time and space, John L. Bell   140
Inspired by love and anger, John L. Bell and Graham Maule   141
Sing praise to God on mountain tops, John L. Bell and Graham Maule   143
Ageless God of boundless wonder, John L. Bell   144
The truth that sets us free, John L. Bell   145
Friends of Jesus, partnered with life, David J.M. Coleman   146
Sources of hymns and songs   147

Resources   149

Links to faith-based community websites relating to the climate crisis   150
CNN-Enviro members' favourite Wild Goose books/downloads   153
CNN-Enviro members' favourite websites   154

About the cover photo

This photo is of a mountain hare I encountered most of the way up the Cobbler (Ben Arthur), in Scotland. I'm really delighted the culling of these creatures is ending.

David J.M. Coleman

Foreword

How do we begin to live faithfully in the time of creation? This collection offers inspiration, ideas and resources to set and sustain us on that path. More than that, we are offered here a synthesis of prayer and action for the sake of all that lives, and for our own life's journey. Each essay offers rich stimulus for considered conversation and action. The liturgical material opens up routes to reflection, contemplation and prayer.

This action/contemplation dynamic is one affirmed at every level within the Iona Community, most recently by a group of young volunteers at our Abbey Centre on Iona, who reminded me that what drew them to work with the Iona Community is the inextricable link they find between prayerful expressions of the Christian faith and action for social justice, world peace and the integrity of creation. This volume leads us deeply, wisely and with care on that journey. I commend Kathy Galloway, Katharine Preston and the whole team of writers – members, associates and friends of the Iona Community from across the world – for their courage and vision as they lead us on this path.

In the book you will meet lament, grief and rage. You will also encounter hope. In the crucible of this volume, lament, anger and rage are welcomed, finding transformation through courageous actions for justice and a fairer world. 2021 is the year that world leaders gather in Glasgow for the 26th 'Conference of the Parties' focusing on collective actions for climate justice. This gathering focuses our hearts and minds on what matters most deeply in our world, and galvanises us to action.

To live faithfully in the time of creation in 2021 and beyond means recognising that the grip of the global pandemic, while releasing levels of compassion and care across the world, is also revealing a deep greed and sense of entitlement as vaccines are locked into wealth and power. It means recognising the inextricable link between the drought, flood and fire that ravage crops, displacing millions of people and species, and the wars and conflict that breed terror in those very same nations. To live faithfully in the time of creation means ordinary citizens being supported and encouraged to continue to welcome our deepest longings, fears and rage and to ask: what am I, what are we now being called to do? How are we now being called to be in this one unique world, as individuals, and in community with the whole of creation?

Ruth Harvey, Leader of the Iona Community

Introduction

Although some of us knew each other, for others, the faces displayed on our screens last autumn were meeting for the first time. It was the first Zoom call for the Iona Community's newly formed Common Concern Network – Environment (CCN-Enviro).[1] Our moderator, Ran Nisbett, from Alabama, USA, was faced with the task of organising a motley group of representatives from four continents.

Wonderful to be together, eye to eye, but … what was next?

We knew, indeed, we did have 'common concerns'. Many of us have been involved with environmental justice in one way or another for decades. We are steeped in a love for the natural world and concern for the threats to it, and to those marginalised people who are bearing the brunt of the effects of the climate emergency.

Our Iona Community Rule is clear: we need to work *'for justice and peace, wholeness and reconciliation in our localities, society and the whole creation'.*[2] But what could a group from across Europe, America, Africa and Australia actually *do* together to further our commitment and address our climate emergency?

Fairly quickly, COP26 (the United Nations Conference of the Parties, 26th Climate Change Conference), rescheduled from 2020 to the autumn of 2021 in Glasgow, presented itself as an opportunity not to be missed. The Iona Community's base is in Glasgow and faith communities throughout Scotland and the rest of the UK were already seeking ways to become involved.

What unique contribution could the Iona Community, via its CCN-Enviro, offer? Wild Goose Publications and the Wild Goose Resource Group are the most publicly visible aspects of the Community's work, so a publication with liturgical and other resources for churches came to mind. A 'Season of Creation', traditional to some communities of faith, conveniently preceded the COP26 meetings, forming a specific timetable.

Thus, *Living Faithfully in the Time of Creation* was born. As members of the CCN-Enviro and as two writers always happy to engage with other writers, we offered to shepherd this book through the initial editing process.

We are blessed to have had more than 20 contributors, including some from other regions of the world, willing to write reflections on scripture or essays. Working with them revealed vital new perspectives on the challenges facing the world. We also asked John Bell and Jo Love of the Wild Goose Resource Group to create a new liturgy that could be used during the 'Season of Creation', through the weeks of COP26, and that could also be adapted in future years.

We gathered together appropriate liturgical resources and sought out websites throughout the world to provide further guidance on actions that could be undertaken by local faith communities in response to the climate emergency.

There is a great deal to do and not much time in which to do it. We pray this small volume provides strands of hope and motivation for you to live faithfully during all seasons, joining other brothers and sisters across the world seeking a community of willing reconciliation with the planet.

Kathy Galloway (UK) and Katharine M. Preston (USA), on behalf of the Iona Community's Common Concern Network – Environment, April 2021

Notes

1. The Iona Community Common Concern Network:
   https://iona.org.uk/about-us/concerns

2. The Rule of the Iona Community:
   https://iona.org.uk/movement/the-rule

Lectionary reflections

Introduction

'This is the season for letting our prayer be inspired anew by closeness to nature … to reflect on our lifestyles … for undertaking prophetic actions … directing the planet towards life, not death.' (Pope Francis)

The following reflections are offered as commentary on the Lectionary texts given in the Revised Common Lectionary, Year B, for the last twelve Sundays of the Season after Pentecost. They commence on the 15th Sunday after Pentecost and continue through until the Last Sunday after Pentecost (Reign of Christ), which is also the last Sunday of the Christian Year, and of Year B. They have a particular focus on creation.

In 2021, these Sundays cover the widely observed Creation Time period (15th–19th Sundays after Pentecost), and the period leading up to, and immediately following, the 26th UN Climate Change Conference of the Parties (COP26), which is due to take place in Glasgow, Scotland, from 1st–12th November 2021. This meeting brings governments from around the world together to discuss action on climate change, at a crucial time for planetary health and human well-being.

As a Christian community with its origins and mainland base in Glasgow, and a commitment to environmental justice as part of our membership Rule of Life, the Iona Community decided to publish a worship book particularly focusing on the climate emergency, which could serve churches, faith groups and individuals. Though not specifically about COP26, we hope that this book will act as a resource for people far beyond Scotland, as our member-ship now is. The whole world will be affected by the outcomes of COP26.

The book has been prepared and edited by members and friends of the Iona Community's Common Concern Network on the Environment. We hope it will be of use for worship leaders and preachers, as well as for individual reflection and prayer. All those who have written reflections are experienced preachers, from different Christian denominations and in different parts of the world. They have either chosen to reflect on a particular selection from the texts, or from the texts as a whole. The Bible version used is the New Revised Standard Version; the Revised Common Lectionary shares much of its content with other commonly used lectionaries, and the reflections will be equally valid in the future.

Kathy Galloway

15th Sunday after Pentecost (B)

Reading

If a brother or sister is naked and lacks daily food, and one of you says to them, 'Go in peace; keep warm and eat your fill,' and yet you do not supply their bodily needs, what is the good of that? So faith by itself, if it has no works, is dead.

(James 2:15–17, NRSV)

Reflection

This isn't about 'earning salvation', an impossible task. It's about showing how our faith and belief affect our behaviour. We are following Jesus and trying to put what he taught into practice, not hoping a supernatural hand will fix everything. Praying and then trying to be part of the answer to prayer. Grateful that God loves us unconditionally but wanting to do our best for the one who knows what we are capable of and understands our limitations. Loving our neighbour as ourselves.

Most in the UK are used to seeing shop shelves full of food. Whether we can afford what we need or want is an important but separate issue. Whether the food is good for us isn't always the point, although of course it matters. We assume the food will be there and complain if it isn't. How long would it take for complaint to turn to understandable panic?

In spring 2020 the island of Mull off the west coast of Scotland received a one-off large delivery of food from FareShare, the charity which redistributes surplus food via other charities. The non-perishable food was destined for the newly established foodbank. But there was enough fresh fruit and veg that a high proportion of households received a good-sized bag; nothing to do with whether we could or couldn't afford it but because, in the early days of lockdown when more people were trying to shop without leaving the island, most shops were struggling to source enough fresh produce.

Mull has lots of green space, some of which is wild and could appropriately be wilder, some of which is grazed by sheep, cows and deer. A few people keep poultry but none on a big enough scale to supply the shops. Local meat, fish, seafood, cheese, biscuits, jams, honey, wool, etc. are available at a fair price for what it takes to produce them, but with some exceptions more expensive than many can afford as a norm. And not in enough quantity if everyone did want to buy them. Many ingredients need to come from elsewhere. A little local veg is available for sale in season and a good number grow some of their own. Home-growing increased a fair bit during 2020. The potential for growing in unused and underused spaces is big in cities; it is huge in the countryside. Around the country, box schemes are getting more popular. Various commendable initiatives are growing food specifically to supply foodbanks. It would be even better if more were to be grown to sell at affordable prices. Tackling the need for foodbanks is a separate issue.

It's not that long ago since most rural residents would have been growing a high proportion of their staple food. It was often a struggle and nobody would choose to go back to the hardship involved. But we're at the other extreme. With the increased knowledge and support available we could turn the proportions around and produce most of our own food, while importing and exporting some treats. Why are we importing herbs from Africa which can be grown all year round in this country? Why are we exporting seafood which could be eaten closer to home? It's a system which has served some well and provided employment. Systems can change and still do both these things. The result: drastic reduction in carbon footprint, in pesticides and fertiliser, in waste, in packaging and pollution. Drastic increase in healthy soil, biodiversity, local composting, animal welfare, human health, satisfying work, planetary hope. Have faith and sow some seeds.

Question

Which countries does your food come from? Could any of it be produced closer to home? If yes, why isn't it?

Action

Plan a meal with ingredients all sourced from the country you live in. Share the meal plan more widely, along with any particular challenges it posed or surprises it contained.

Prayer

God of all the world,
we give thanks for the variety of food and drink
we have enjoyed in our lives,
grateful for the hard work which has fed so many for so long,
acknowledging the cost to people and planet of unsustainable production.
Inspire vision and grant courage to find different ways forward,
learning from the past, excited for the future, caring in the present.
Combine our faith and works to bring life in its fullness for all the world.

Liz Gibson

Liz Gibson and her husband, Martyn, have lived on a croft on Mull, now certified organic, since 2013. With the help of volunteers, they have planted native hedging, fruit trees, herbs and annual vegetables, as well as establishing Isle of Mull Tea. Liz is a minister ordained in the Church of Scotland and a member of the Iona Community. She is now parish minister for North Mull.

16th Sunday after Pentecost (B)

Reading

Wisdom cries out in the street;
*   in the squares she raises her voice.*
At the busiest corner she cries out;
*   at the entrance of the city gates she speaks:*
'How long, O simple ones, will you love being simple?
How long will scoffers delight in their scoffing
*   and fools hate knowledge?*
Give heed to my reproof;
I will pour out my thoughts to you
*   I will make my words known to you …*

but those who listen to me will be secure
*   and will live at ease, without dread of disaster.'*

(Proverbs 1:20–23, 33, NRSV)

Reflection

For a long time, I avoided what we used to call the 'Old Testament'. It seemed to be full of images of an angry, vindictive God who punishes people for their wrongdoings and sins. And then one day I looked at it again, and it spoke to me. I saw the Hebrew Bible with completely new eyes. We are not punished for our sins, but *by* our sins, by the consequences of our actions! I have learned to read the biblical language differently. It is not about God coming down and punishing us; it is about our actions – and inaction – causing harm to ourselves, to other people, to our common home, our planet. God does not want that! We read in Ezekiel 33:1: *Say to them, As I live, says the Lord God, I have no pleasure in the death of the wicked, but that the wicked turn from their ways and live; turn back, turn back from your evil ways …*

As an example, let us look at the forests of my adopted home, Scotland. Or rather – let us have a look at their history:

'Woodland cover around 5,000 years ago reached Shetland and the Western Isles … then began to decline, largely due to early agriculture. By the time the Roman legions of Agricola invaded Scotland in AD 82, at least half of our natural wood-

land had gone. Much of it was replaced by peatland, partly as a result of the cooler, wetter climate and partly because of human activities ...

By 1900, woodland covered only about 5% of Scotland's land area, as many small and isolated blocks. This led to the loss of species requiring larger, unbroken blocks of native woodland – especially larger mammals and predators. [1]

The deforestation in Scotland that had begun long before our time was dramatically accelerated from the 18th century onwards: by the Clearances, by agricultural and industrial revolutions and by the development of large shooting estates,[2] all driven to maximise profit, and resulting in too many cows and sheep, the overpopulation of deer, and in many places, almost no wild nature left. The only natural source of drinking water on one of the islands I know well is no longer fit for use.

Today, there are wonderful reforestation projects already at work. Forests are the lungs of our planet, each precious tree, each little plant produces the oxygen we breathe and consumes the CO2 we emit. We need them – we need them to be able to live.

We can find a new harmony with creation, if we are willing to listen to the groaning of the world. We need to stop the destruction by reducing our carbon emissions, by considering the environment in every decision that we make, and by planting trees again.

In Jewish tradition (and in many Christian traditions too) Wisdom, She who cries out in the streets in the Proverbs text, is one of the images, one of the attempts, used to describe the nature of God. It tells us about a loving God who cares deeply about the whole of the wonderful, diverse, rich creation – including us. We are not above creation, not meant to subdue and exploit it as has been done for a very long time. Instead we are part of it, intertwined: one thread of the fragile mesh of life. But we are destroying it. With our greed, our consumerism, our poor sharing and poor care, we are polluting the waters and the air and the earth we depend on for life. We are contributing to climate catastrophe. It is injustice against our planet and injustice against the people who suffer most from it. We are cutting a hole in the very boat that carries us and our children through the sea of life. And we are diminishing the beauty of the world's diversity at the same time.

Let us listen to Wisdom, to God! Let us change our ways and live, have a life and a future for our planet, for our beautiful fellow creatures and for our children. It's almost too late, but not quite. Turn around now, repent now, change our ways now – as individuals and as society! Let us make wise, informed choices in our everyday lives; let us raise awareness and work to change the destructive systems and mechanisms in our societies.

Prayer

Source of all life,
God of the lush forests,
God of the clean air,
God of the clear waters,
God of every living creature,
open our eyes, minds and hearts
to see that we are all connected,
all part of the same network of life:
what hurts and pollutes one,
hurts and pollutes the other.

Help us to listen to you
and to repent from our destructive ways.
So that your wonderful, diverse planet
can breathe again and live,
and we and our children with it.
Amen.

Question

Ask your church or community when and how they plan to go 'net zero' (the UK government has committed itself to cutting greenhouse gas emissions to 'net zero' by 2050).[3] Keep asking until it happens. Inform yourself about the best ways to lower the CO_2 footprint.

Action

Find out which trees are best suited to the changing climate in your area and, if possible, endemic. Then find a way to plant one or several of them. Connect with reforestation organisations.

Urzula Glienecke

Urzula Glienecke, PhD, is a member of the Iona Community and a Latvian theologian, artist and activist living in Scotland (https://artseekingmeaning.com). She has worked and studied in Latvia, Norway, Germany, Spain, the Republic of Ireland and Scotland and has travelled around the world. She is passionate about working together with people on the margins and preserving our diverse and wonderful environment.

Notes

1. From 'History of Scotland's woodlands' on the NatureScot: Scotland's Nature Agency website, www.nature.scot

2. Information from 'History of Scotland's woodlands', NatureScot: Scotland's Nature Agency website, www.nature.scot

3. See:
   https://www.instituteforgovernment.org.uk/sites/default/files/publications/net-zero-government-climate-change-target.pdf

Fragile creation

Sculpture, by Urzula Glienecke ©

Photo, by Michael Glienecke ©

17th Sunday after Pentecost (B)

Reading

He sat down, called the twelve, and said to them, 'Whoever wants to be first must be last of all and servant of all.' Then he took a little child and put it among them; and taking it in his arms, he said to them, 'Whoever welcomes one such child in my name welcomes me, and whoever welcomes me welcomes not me but the one who sent me.'

(Mark 9:35–37, NRSV)

Reflection

The mountains of Eryri (Snowdonia), North Wales, can teach humility and perspective if we are willing to learn. It can be a harsh landscape with unforgiving rocks, and a grittiness of daily life. It is also possible, of course, to catch a glimpse of divine beauty. The strength and determination of the natural world can encourage us to continue on in the face of difficult times. If one is humble enough to respect natural limits, we can learn. Nature can flourish here offering immense beauty as we experience the interaction of sunlight with the environment. Each new moment offers perspectives which warm the heart and touch the soul. This is not a romantic vision; rather, it is a narrow way, a fragile gap between life and death as on a mountain precipice, but also in everyday life. Life is fragile here and humans need to learn to live in balance.

In Mark's Gospel Jesus speaks of humility in being servant of all.

As we attempt to follow Jesus's way, serving our sisters and brothers, can we be servant of the ecological environment as well? Allowing human needs and wants to come second is not natural for us and to do this we need new perspectives. We need to find ways to listen to the cry of the earth. Jesus offers us the image of a child being welcomed in our midst. When we truly welcome someone, we accept them for who they are, welcoming their ideas, thoughts and perspectives. Do we welcome a child as one who needs to grow and learn, or as someone from whom we can learn as we watch and develop with them over the years?

The perspective of a child is as one close to the earth, literally. Often looking up, but also out at that level. Tall grass might not be knee height, but head height. This natural closeness to nature is something adults have, sadly, learnt to grow out of. The mind of a child offers a perspective that can often shed adult illusions. A child is also one who will grow and live beyond our years. Can we honour that future in our actions towards children and towards the earth?

The global COP26 meeting is the latest attempt to confront and mitigate the worst effects of consumerism, globalisation and the Industrial Revolution. We are still overly reliant on fossil fuels, pumping more carbon into the atmosphere than the earth can naturally mitigate. In these attempts to reduce our footprint, how often do we even try to listen to the voice of the earth itself? Much like the child teaching humility to Jesus's disciples, could we learn from the very hills and mountains, rivers and valleys that have been so polluted? The earth from whom we believed we could take without limit or ignore out of hand could be the one to whom we could turn to listen for a new perspective. This is nothing new. 'Nature-based solutions' are an attempt to listen to the voice of that which has been here millennia before us and will still be long after our departure. They are designed to build human capacity to adapt to climate change, working alongside the natural world, rather than against it.[1]

Jesus teaches us to be humble. In terms of the environmental situation we find ourselves in, that means putting human concerns lower than the wider ecological needs. Jesus suggests the practice of welcoming children. This means truly accepting their perspective without prejudice to their age or learning. In terms of the environmental situation, are we willing to pay attention to the perspective of children and, through their eyes, to what the natural world has been telling us for so long?

Prayer

God, you were not afraid to be humble. Help us to confront the fears that hold us back from listening to new voices, living in your ways and acting to sustain your world. Amen.

Question

When we face an ecological issue, how often do we first listen, watch and learn from nature?

Action

Practise humility by leaving to nature a small patch of ground in your care. Watch and learn from what goes on.

Stuart Elliott

Stuart Elliott is a priest in the Church in Wales living in Eryri (Snowdonia), North Wales. He writes and speaks regularly about the climate crisis and nature connection. When not tending to his flock (people, not sheep!), he can often be found running in the hills. Stuart is an associate member of the Iona Community.

Note

1. See www.naturebasedsolutionsinitiative.org/what-are-nature-based-solutions

18th Sunday after Pentecost (B)

Reading

John said to him, 'Teacher, we saw someone casting out demons in your name, and we tried to stop him, because he was not following us.' But Jesus said, 'Do not stop him; for no one who does a deed of power in my name will be able soon afterward to speak evil of me. Whoever is not against us is for us. For truly I tell you, whoever gives you a cup of water to drink because you bear the name of Christ will by no means lose the reward.

'If any of you put a stumbling block before one of these little ones who believe in me, it would be better for you if a great millstone were hung around your neck and you were thrown into the sea. If your hand causes you to stumble, cut it off; it is better for you to enter life maimed than to have two hands and to go to hell, to the unquenchable fire. And if your foot causes you to stumble, cut it off; it is better for you to enter life lame than to have two feet and to be thrown into hell. And if your eye causes you to stumble, tear it out; it is better for you to enter the kingdom of God with one eye than to have two eyes and to be thrown into hell, where their worm never dies, and the fire is never quenched.

'For everyone will be salted with fire. Salt is good; but if salt has lost its saltiness, how can you season it? Have salt in yourselves, and be at peace with one another.'

(Mark 9:38–50, NRSV)

Reflection

Was Jesus serious with his talk about cutting off limbs and tearing out eyes? Or was he joking? The answer surely is 'both'.

Jesus' talk was laced with exaggeration and parable and that's what we have here. But like his parable of the crazy farmer who throws his seed on the rocks and the path, or the person who puts a lamp under a bushel, he has a serious point. Deadly serious.

Jesus' time was a time of crisis. A critical hour. Like ours.

The so-called *Pax Romana* was built on violence and maintained by violence. From the cruelty of the circus to the brutality of the armies, from the increasing wealth of the few to the desperate poverty of the many, from the luxury of the landowners to the slaves in the fields and mines, there was structural violence.

There were people who wanted to use violence to overthrow it. But, as Jesus said, 'Those who live by the sword die by the sword.' Insurrections were punished with crucifixions. In due course, rebellions in Palestine led to the destruction of Jerusalem and the despairing deaths at Masada.

Jesus' way was another way. Creative love.

'The reign of God is at hand,' he said. As he healed the sick and exorcised demons the reign of God was visible. And people either aligned with God's creative love or worked against it. That was the choice.

In our time structural violence more obviously extends to our environment: to the insects, the animals, the forests and the ice caps, as well as to people. Rains fail in East Africa. Storms rage in North America. Floods wipe out farms and homes in South Asia. Mass industrialisation feeds the appetites of those who can pay and impoverishes those who cannot.

But the reign of God is still at hand. It is God's creation that is being damaged, and God continues to be at work. Where there is healing, where demons are cast out, and where people live with the creative love of God, the reign of God is visible.

And there are surprises. Whoever wants to be first must be last. The servant is the greatest. Children are the ambassadors. And it is not only those who are part of Jesus' obvious group who are on his side. 'Whoever is not against us is for us,' he said.

As it was to Jesus' Galilean hearers, the challenge to us is which side we will be on. Will we be with God or against God? Will we join the movement to bring healing to the world? To exorcise the demons of consumption? To let slaves be free? To care for the world that is our children's inheritance? To encourage the hopes of the poor and not to dash them?

To do so we may need to get rid of something that causes us to stumble and so holds us back.

To Jesus' hearers 'hands and feet' spoke about what they did. Maybe we need to change what we do. Stop flying? Drive less? Ride a bike? Change our diet? Maybe our changes need to be about what we do with our skills, our time or our money. Perhaps we need to keep less for ourselves and give more to organisations who work to help the world's poorest, or plant trees, or campaign for structural change.

To Jesus' hearers, 'eyes' were about how they thought and made decisions. Maybe our changes need to be more about how we look at the world. Ask who is benefitting from the way the world operates. Who is losing out? What it is doing to our environment? To the climate?

This might change how we think, how we feel, what we say, and how we vote.

To Jesus' hearers losing an eye, a hand, or a foot removed you from the company of wholesome people and put you among the beggars. It changed your status.

Perhaps the changes we need to make, the things we need to say or do, will alter how people see us, think about us or feel about us, and move us into different company.

But that's the challenge. It's serious.

Prayer

God, you call the world into being
and hold it in love,
your Spirit heals its wounds
and renews its life,
Jesus shows us your ways
and invites us to follow;
help us to reject what deceives us,
discard what hinders us,
and ignore what distracts us,
so that with grace and freedom
we may share more fully in your eternal life.

David Osborne

David Osborne is a member of the Iona Community living in Somerset, England. He has been at various times an engineer, a teacher and a vicar. He is the author of Love for the Future: A Journey *(Wild Goose Publications) and of a Living Spirituality Connections course: www.livingspirit.org.uk/lftf/course-introduction.*

19th Sunday after Pentecost (B)

Reading

Long ago God spoke to our ancestors in many and various ways by the prophets ...

(Hebrews 1:1–4, 2:5–12, NRSV)

Reflection

Frequently, children and the future frame debates around climate change. Certainly, the lectionary passages appeal to this image today. Brazil is a young country with many young people. However, its religious traditions are old. The *mística*[1] and the ancestral traditions and voices from indigenous and African religious traditions mix with the prophetic religions of Christianity, Islam and Judaism.

The lectionary passages appeal to an image of the past, too. Genealogies and ancestral lines appear throughout the biblical canon. Biblical genealogies and ancestral lines focus on an understanding of faith and the world as a human history transmitted through the generations. Moreover, of course, the generations are measured in human life spans.

Climate change and climate justice invite us to consider genealogies and ancestral lines in an understanding wider than 'human history'. Geological ages shape our biblical genealogies and our ancestral faith. Climate change and climate justice also profoundly challenge the prophetic religions' human-centred story of salvation.

The South African theologian Ernst Conradie invites us to shift from an anthropological theology to a cosmological theology when addressing climate change. Without a theology which contemplates the cosmos and the human place within the cosmos, Conradie argues, it is all too easy for theology to blindly assume the medieval hierarchy of God – humans – natural world where each 'acts' upon the other. God acts on humans. Humans act in the natural world in a descending order of importance. Conradie prefers to advocate for an interdependent understanding of our cosmos. Geology is not subordinate to human history, and the story of salvation is not 'save our planet to save ourselves (or even our children's children)'.[2]

Christianity in Brazil is deeply impacted by narratives of conquest. The conquering of the Americas, the conquering of souls for Christ, the conquering of the flesh by the spirit, and so on. Conradie's proposal, and the wider challenge from climate change and climate justice, is for Christianity to change its narrative to one of co-operation: co-operation with the cosmos, co-operation with other religions, and co-operation with other genealogies and ancestors. In *Homage to the American Indians*, the Nicaraguan poet, priest and politician, Ernesto Cardenal, wrote about listening to the ancestral voices of the trees, the stones and the waters.[3]

The debate and action about climate change is about the future; it is also about the past. We are invited to discover the many and varied ways that God spoke to our cosmological ancestors.

Collect

Earth God,
we are of the Earth.
We honour the Earth as a place of living beings.
We praise the Earth for its beauty and biodiversity.
We recognise a shared responsibility to care for,
restore and replenish the Earth.
Speak to us through the Earth, now and forever.

(Based on *The Letter of the Earth*, Rio 1992)

Question

Who are our ancestors? Do the trees, the stones and the waters transmit the faith through geological ages?

Action

I live beside the beach. We have a collection of shells. On holding each shell to our ear, we hear a different sound or voice. Find a place to sit in your own environment. What noises do you hear? Which of those noises do you associate with climate change and which with climate justice? Is there any action that you can take to change the sounds of your environment?

Graham McGeoch

Graham McGeoch is a minister of the Church of Scotland. He lives in Brazil and teaches Theology & Religious Studies at Faculdade Unida de Vitória.

Notes

1. 'The Brazilian Landless Workers Movement (MST) works to create solidarity and collective identity among its members through a variety of pedagogical practices. One such practice is *mística*, which is at once a public, expressive dramatic performance and, drawing on Christian mysticism, a way of making contact with a transcendent reality. *Mística* draws on Christian theology generally, and specifically on the practices of the Christian base communities associated with liberation theology which were key in the emergence of the MST. It fortifies activists with the high commitment needed to engage in land occupations and the creation of farming communities through which the MST pursues its central goal of agrarian reform.'

   From *Mística, meaning and popular education in the Brazilian Landless Workers Movement*, by John L Hammond, www.mstbrazil.org

2. *An Ecological Christian Anthropology: At Home on Earth?*, Ernst M Conradie, Routledge, 2017

3. *Homage to the American Indians*, Ernesto Cardenal, Johns Hopkins University Press, 1973

20th Sunday after Pentecost (B)

Reading

Then Job answered:

'Today also my complaint is bitter;
  his hand is heavy despite my groaning.
Oh, that I knew where I might find him,
  that I might come even to his dwelling!'

(Job 23:1–3, NRSV)

Let us therefore approach the throne of grace with boldness, so that we may receive mercy and find grace to help in time of need.

(Hebrews 4:16, NRSV)

Jesus looked at them and said, 'For mortals it is impossible, but not for God; for God all things are possible.'

(Mark 10:27, NRSV)

Reflection

Job is grieving, rightly so as he has had so many disasters inflicted on him. In this rabbinic story about suffering, Job is wanting justice and to be heard by God. We know that grieving has many aspects, from anger and tears, denial and confusion, to that strange search for the one you love and lost. In your head you know they have died, but something within doesn't quite believe it and you visit different places they have been in the past, as if to check they are not there.

Some years ago I gathered contributions for a book of liturgies, stories and essays about creation: God's Big Book, as I prefer to think of it. Most of the contributions were about lament, a grieving for what was happening in creation. There was a lot of blame and some denial addressed in the book, both aspects of grieving. We still see this denial of climate change, even in prominent politicians. However, numerous TV and radio programmes on the natural world, and particularly about the state of the sea due to our use of plastic, have alerted us to the mess we have created. We do now know that change is necessary, particularly in the Western lifestyle, so it's natural there are aspects of grieving about.

Mixed in with grief is guilt. We did not know that industrialisation, begun centuries ago, would cause damage to the planet. We cannot be blamed for what happened then. But now we *do* know that change is needed, and there have been some encouraging and creative changes in the production of green electricity, just as an example. Both grief and guilt can cause human beings to freeze in their actions; they need to be addressed to free up the creativity and imagination that will help us make the necessary changes.

The epistle gives us the clue. We cannot hide our secret thoughts and wishes from God: God knows everything about us. However, because Jesus has shown us the deep and unending love of God, we know we are forgiven. We can approach God with boldness, knowing that God will be with us and inspire us. We can offer God the sadness and guilt we feel for the wrong done to God's Big Book, for that transforming love of God to free us from inaction and wrong action, to right action.

We are resistant though. I've been in many conversations about the environment where it is clear most people want change, but not for them! We are like that rich young ruler who wanted to follow Jesus, stuck when lifestyle changes seemed too daunting. But look at what he missed! Life as a disciple of Jesus, the Messiah! We have enjoyed the bounty and wealth of creation; we have often used creation regardless of the impact. Now creation needs our help, and it is time to face into the grief and guilt that prevent us from acting. It is time to say sorry and really mean it, so that the situation changes. It is also time to recognise that individuals can indeed make an important difference, but unless corporations change it will not be enough. Every government, every corporation, every business has to make the necessary changes to the way they operate. They need to benefit creation and reduce the greedy footprint of past decades. As a very simple example, it does not benefit creation if the recycling of individual households is not actually recycled into something else by the refuse industry. Worse if it is just dumped in other countries.

It is worth all the struggle. Not just for the younger generations and those yet to be born, but for ourselves. Maundy Thursday and Good Friday had to be lived through for Easter to dawn. There will be gifts for us from the changes society has to make, perhaps a gentler and kinder way of life. I am sure of this: care for God's creation which sustains us will have gifts that are now only on the edges of our dreams.

Prayer

Living God,
your Big Book of creation is so amazing –
the detail, the connectedness of all things;
thank you for the beauty around us.
We are sorry for the damage we have done,
and need your help to change well.
Free us from all that prevents us
from caring for the earth and each other.
So we live gently on earth
and all creation praises you.

Question

In your life so far, how has knowing Jesus changed you, your group, your church?

Action

Write a lament either for the climate change consequences that most concern you, or for the lifestyle changes that trouble you.

Chris Polhill

Chris Polhill is a member of the Iona Community and the author of A Heart for Creation: Worship Resources and Reflections on the Environment *(Wild Goose Publications). In 1999, Chris and her husband, John, bought a home on the edge of Cannock Chase (20 miles north of Birmingham). In the grounds of this property they have created a series of themed gardens on the Christian spiritual journey and environmental issues. The gardens and meeting space/retreat accommodation are used regularly by individuals and groups (www.reflectiongardens.org.uk).*

21st Sunday after Pentecost (B)

Reading

Then the Lord *answered Job out of the whirlwind:*

'Who is this that darkens counsel by words without knowledge? ...'

(Job 38:1–2, NRSV)

Reflection

If you look west from the hilltops of Jerusalem and Bethlehem, you can see the saffron-coloured Jordanian hills rising out of the Dead Sea. But there are days when the sky turns incarnadine, and dust and sand particles fill the air and obstruct the view. The wind picks up and blows through this beautiful and yet conflicted land ravaged by the injustice of military occupation, checkpoints and walls, that keep people apart and entrench division. This is a land of both hope and broken dreams.

In today's Old Testament lectionary reading from Job 38, God answers Job from out of the whirlwind. But what is so striking about this piece of Hebrew poetry is that God does not so much answer Job's questions by giving him the responses he is looking for about why there is suffering in our world. Instead, God's answers come in the form of questions: *'Where were you when I laid the foundation of the earth?'* (v.4). *'Who determined its measurements?'* (v.5). *'Who has put wisdom in the inward parts, or given understanding to the mind?'* (v.36). This tradition of answering by question is prevalent throughout the Hebrew Scriptures, and was the tradition Christ was to draw on when teaching his parables. More often than not, Jesus answered by asking questions.

In our post-scientific age, where the world and our knowledge of it has become domesticated and documented, we at times find it difficult to live with the questions. We crave after sound bites, and answers we can access at the tap of our fingers, in a world where information overload is king. But the journey of faith is not something that can be rationally explained and empirically categorised, but only comes alive when we open ourselves up to the mystery of God, who doesn't usually appear in clarity, but speaks from within the whirlwind of our doubts, questions and fears, as she did to Job, and doesn't come with easy answers. Instead, we are invited to be drawn up into the timeless mystery of God's love, in this passage depicted as set against the awe-inspiring majesty and wonder of nature.

In verse 4 we read that it is God who *'laid the foundation of the earth'*, and She did so in love, for God is love, and God is the possibility of love in such a world as ours, a world ravaged by structural injustice and war, ecological devastation and violence. But the picture of creation captured in this passage depicts a universe at peace with itself, evoking stars that *'sang together'* and heavenly beings that *'shouted for joy'* (v.7). It is a far cry from the devastation we see in our broken world today, ravaged by greed over-consumption, by war and conflict.

In Israel Palestine where I live and minister, the militarised networks of occupation force themselves onto hilltops where shepherds once grazed, and scar through the land with watchtowers, barbed wire and walls. The land where Job cried out from the midst of suffering still cries out today. The land where our suffering God took on human form, with us and amongst us in vulnerability and outpoured love, now comes to heal, restore and make new, and invites us to be a part of the healing of our fragile world.

In Dostoevsky's novel *The Brothers Karamazov* it says that *'the world will be saved through beauty'*. Beauty has come into our world. Beauty is always vulnerable. It is always fragile. The God of Job comes to our suffering world and invites us on a journey of mystery and faith. She summons us from the clouds of unknowing and the whirling storms of life, reminding us that She enfolds creation in her love, and invites us to do the same.

Prayer

God of the cloud,
God of the storm,
sweep into our troubled hearts
and ravaged world
with the healing touch
of your renewal and grace.

And may we be your
hands and feet,
bringing beauty and justice
in your broken world.
Amen.

Question

How can we re-imagine our neighbourhoods, cities and world through the eyes of beauty? How can we plant seeds of rebirth in our barren wastelands?

Action

Visit the website of the Joint Advocacy Initiative in Bethlehem, and sponsor the planting of an olive tree deep within the Occupied West Bank:

www.jai-pal.org/en

John McCulloch

John McCulloch is the Church of Scotland minister of St Andrew's Jerusalem & Tiberias in the Holy Land. His ministry takes him across Israel and the Occupied Palestinian Territories. Prior to responding to the call into ministry, he was a lecturer in Hispanic Studies at Glasgow University.

22nd Sunday after Pentecost (B)

Reading

Then Job answered the LORD:

'I know that you can do all things,
  and that no purpose of yours can be thwarted.
"Who is this that hides counsel without knowledge?"
Therefore I have uttered what I did not understand,
  things too wonderful for me, which I did not know.
"Hear, and I will speak;
  I will question you, and you declare to me."
I had heard of you by the hearing of the ear,
  but now my eye sees you;
therefore I despise myself,
  and repent in dust and ashes.'

(Job 42:1–6, NRSV)

Then Jesus said to him, 'What do you want me to do for you?' The blind man said to him, 'My teacher, let me see again.'

(Mark 10:51, NRSV)

Reflection

The Book of Job could well be subtitled 'The chastening of Job!'. It is one of the most painful lessons of adulthood, realising how little we really know, and how much less we can command. The struggle to impose our will on everything around us, including the earth, causes grave damage to the environment, to other people and to ourselves.

Job was being called to let God be God. Even with all our scientific insight, what we know about the universe is so much less than what is still mysterious to us. The natural order in all its complexity and beauty moved a quantum physicist to say that the appropriate response to it is one of sheer wonder and love. But such a celebration requires the dethronement of human ego, and the birth of co-operation with nature rather than domination over it.

I live in Scotland, a country with a long history of fossil fuel extraction. The history, extent and impact of mining in Scotland has been extraordinary, transformational and in some regards, dreadful. Tens of thousands of men, women and children worked in mining, and it has been estimated that at the beginning of the 20th century, almost one million Scots were directly or indirectly dependent on the industry. My own family were among them; I come from four generations of West Lothian coal and shale-oil miners. Coal fuelled the Industrial Revolution. Modernity depended as much upon mining as it did upon the Enlightenment. In the last half-century, North Sea oilfields have been drivers of prosperity.

My mining forebears did not become rich through mining. They lived in squalid conditions, their work was dirty, dangerous and sometimes fatal, their health cruelly compromised by their occupation. The rights and rewards available to them for their labour, notwithstanding its essential value to their country and people, seem remarkably meagre. Nevertheless, their strong communities took pride in the importance of their work, often the only kind available to them to feed their families. They did not know then that they were contributing to the greatest threat to human life on earth, negatively impacting whole ecosystems and accelerating climate change. Like Job, they did not know what they did not know. In their ignorance lay their innocence.

But we are not ignorant. We know about the people at the base of the apex that is the present-day extractives industry in the poorest countries, still working in 19th century conditions. We know about the people whose lives are most affected by its consequences, displaced from degraded land or uprooted from homes and livelihoods by the extreme weather events of climate change and its related conflicts. We know – but do we really see – those pushed out to the edge of our awareness? They are mostly poor; they are mostly people of colour. We are habituated to not seeing them.

When the blind beggar Bartimaeus called to Jesus from the roadside, the crowd following Jesus was hostile, tried to shut him up and keep him out of the way, to make him even less visible than he already was. But Jesus stopped and called Bartimaeus to come to him, and he asked him, 'what do you want me to do for you?' Bartimaeus asks to see again; so that he can support himself and not be a perpetual supplicant, so that he can be restored into human community. And being seen, he sees.

The patient attentiveness of Jesus, his recognition of Bartimaeus's personhood, the dignity he restores by asking him rather than telling him what he needs, is a different way of seeing. It offers a different kind of knowledge, one that does not seek power or profit, but instead offers restoration and life.

Both the Book of Job and Mark's gospel challenge a particular kind of pious orthodoxy, the easy linkage of virtue and prosperity and the equally shallow linkage of sin and suffering. They go beyond cheap grace into painful questions of injustice, beyond theological posturing into the humility of a faith lived at the limits of experience.

And as we struggle with what it will mean for us to leave the fossil fuels in the ground – as we must – shall we also struggle to practise that different way of seeing?

Prayer

God our strength and hope,
may we never take for granted the costs to others
of fossil fuel extraction,
and have the wisdom to know how much they involve us,
in our consumption, in our investments, in our mobility.
Give us your strength to discover new and gentler ways of living.
Give us your hope in the possibility of fullness of life
for all who share the good earth,
that beauty may blossom out of ash.
Amen.

Question

Who do we need to be more attentive to, and how can we do that?

Action

Find out how you, your church, your local government, can stop investing in fossil fuels: your national Friends of the Earth organisation might be a good place to start: www.foei.org

Kathy Galloway

Kathy Galloway is a writer, activist and practical theologian. She has worked for the Iona Community, Christian Aid and Church Action on Poverty. She lives in Glasgow, Scotland.

23rd Sunday after Pentecost (B)

Reading

But when Christ came as a high priest of the good things that have come ...he entered once for all into the Holy Place ... thus obtaining eternal redemption ... who through the eternal Spirit, offered himself without blemish to God, to purify our conscience from dead works to worship the living God!

(Hebrews 9:11, 12, 14, NRSV)

Reflection

What makes a place 'holy'? Is a holy place somewhere like the Ganges or Jerusalem? Is it somewhere beyond the clouds, or a 'thin place' you visit to feel near God?

When Hebrews was written, *the* holy place, the Temple, had been destroyed, but the memory of it had not. It had been the place where God sat amongst God's people. Though the Temple was gone, the faithful continued to make sacrifices at nearby altars, offering what they were able: a pair of doves or some grain. The content of the sacrifice was not nearly as important as the purpose – to offer something of what they had to God. The offering was meant to honour God, emphasise their connection with God, and highlight that what they had was not theirs at all. Everything we have belongs to God. We work, we earn, we create. It is all God's. However, the author of Hebrews assures us, we no longer have to seek out holy places to make sacrifices.

When Christ became the ultimate sacrifice, acting out of God's immense love for all of humanity, it was no longer necessary to travel to holy places to make sacrificial offerings. In Christ, human and divine are one; therefore, we don't need a sacrifice to remind us of our connection. Christ is God-with-us, and, by being with us beyond the Temple, by walking throughout the land, entering the houses of the faithful and the powerful, the lowly and the questionable, Christ dispelled the idea that there is *a* holy place. In Christ, God is no longer constrained to interact with humanity through the priesthood and the Holy of Holies. Now, in Christ, wherever humanity is, is holy. Our lives and our living become a testament to our connection with God, a way of honouring God's love for us, and a witness to the holiness of every place in God's good creation.

Lady Bird Johnson was a woman guided by her faith, who acted to make the world better, more holy, for all. She was a well-educated and successful businesswoman, and charted a new path for the previously honorary role of First Lady when her husband, Lyndon B. Johnson, became President of the United States in November 1963. Her primary platforms were the Civil Rights Act and HeadStart – a programme giving children from low-income families a step up in school readiness. 'Lady Bird' (as she is affectionately known by all Texans) also became a campaigner for the Highway Beautification Act of 1965 – which sought to control advertising, reduce litter and increase the planting of trees and shrubs along the Interstate Highway System.

Back home, she took it a step further and convinced the State of Texas to sow wildflower seeds in highway medians and then allow the flowers to go to seed before they were mown in autumn. Over decades, the small patches have grown into vast swaths of wildflowers. Native birds feast on the native seeds, and Texas children, gazing out the window of the family car on the way to grandma's house, see blue bonnets, Indian paintbrushes, purple coneflower, Texas yellowstar, evening primrose and Indian blankets dancing in the wind of the racing cars.

It is a throwaway place … or it used to be. Now highway medians are treated with respect and the process of seed growth, germination and resowing is honoured almost as though it is holy and that place, too, is holy. By letting the seeds take their course, Lady Bird underscored that even in the midst of concrete and cars, the land belongs to nature … to God. The wildflowers are an offering that highlights that.

Perhaps you do not have the resources or the clout to beautify an entire highway system, but you have the ability to offer your time, energy and efforts as a sacrifice, a reminder that all of creation is God's and, in Christ, wherever humanity is, is holy.

Prayer

God of everyplace,
you are present with me in every moment everywhere.
Help me to see your holiness
on my street, in my town,
in well-manicured, pretty places, and in ugly and neglected places;

so that I can use my resources and skills
to highlight the holiness of this place.
I ask this of the Creator who made me,
through Christ who is with me,
by the Spirit who impels me.
Amen.

Action

Go somewhere you wouldn't consider 'holy' – a busy street, a littered lot, a bus stop. Look around at the place. What do you see? If it is safe, close your eyes. Think about how God created it. Open your eyes and look again. Now, do one thing to highlight the holiness of this place – pick up littler, spread some native wildflower seeds, find out how to work with your city to remove unnecessary pavement and abate graffiti.

Question

If the world itself is a holy place, then how does that change the way you view the beautiful places around you? How about the filthy places?

Liz Johnson Blythe

Liz Johnson Blythe spent many hours as a child, gazing out the car window at Lady Bird's wildflowers on family trips from her home in Dallas, TX. She attended the University of Texas at Austin, earning a Bachelor of Arts in History. After university, Liz worked for two years before attending Princeton Theological Seminary, where she earned a Masters of Divinity. Ordained in the PC (USA), Liz served two churches over 12 years before moving with her family to Glasgow, where she has been serving as locum of a local congregation. She is an associate member of the Iona Community.

24th Sunday after Pentecost (B)

Reading

As he taught, he said, 'Beware of the scribes, who like to walk around in long robes, and to be greeted with respect in the marketplaces, and to have the best seats in the synagogues and places of honour at banquets! They devour widows' houses and for the sake of appearance say long prayers. They will receive the greater condemnation.'

(Mark 12:38–40, NRSV)

Reflection

If a physical gathering is possible, there's going to be a lot of noise around Glasgow in November. Politicians, policymakers, pilgrims and pundits – all hungry for change. The world will converge on our 'Dear Green Place' and the mantra 'People Make Glasgow' will have a chance to prove itself as we embrace our global neighbours. More than a moment, COP26 may be the last real chance we have to change the course our consumerism has set us on. In some ways it is ironic that this summit has come to the United Kingdom, home of the Industrial Revolution, to Scotland, home to James Watt and his remarkable steam engine – our past glories come home to roost. What a marvel, our capacity to create! And what a mess when human creativity clashes, with 'can we do it?' racing ahead of 'should we do it?' Perhaps a call for us all to repent – not a sorrowful weeping and wailing and gnashing of teeth show, but grasping the true, terrifying meaning of repent – turning around and going in an entirely different direction. Not tokenism but transformation.

There's going to be a lot of noise around Glasgow in November, just as there was a lot of noise around Jerusalem and in the Temple. It was Passover and the 'City of Peace' was stormy. Full of priests and pilgrims, politicians, policy-makers and pundits – it was a sea of humanity. And Jesus, in this story from the Gospel of Mark, has been on a collision course with the powers-that-be. Power has a way of finding offence when the truth is close. And Jesus cuts close to the bone: *'Beware of the scribes, who like to walk around in long robes, and to be greeted with respect in the marketplaces, and to have the best seats in the synagogues and places of honour at banquets! They devour widows' houses and for the sake of appearance say long prayers. They will receive the greater condemnation.'*

Jesus is probably referring here to scribes in their role as solicitors or estate guardians. A position of great power, they received a percentage of the value of any estate they managed. They could *'eat up widows' houses'*. They were also appointed to this position, so needed to be seen as holy and above reproach. So, they dressed well, made sure they were visible in all the right places and were heard saying their prayers. In our text, Jesus painted quite the word-portrait!

There was a lot of noise in the Temple, and Jesus was watchful, leaning back and listening to coins being tossed into the treasury chests. It would have made an impressive sound! Called trumpets because of their shape, these metal containers were built for show – and *'many rich people were throwing many coins'* – one by one or handfuls at a time, they rang out with piety! And Jesus points to a widow with two *lepta* – the smallest Palestinian coins that together added up to a *kodrantēs*, Rome's smallest sum. Not much of a noise – she didn't even throw them in, she placed them.

- Many rich people, throwing many coins – making noise with their surplus.

- One widow, and it was all she had – no noise, but it speaks volumes, doesn't it?

When COP comes to Glasgow, the world has possibly its last chance to right a wrong and reach for a better future. Our actions have consumed our shared home and made those with least responsibility for this pay the highest price. We cannot afford for those of us with the most to make noise with our surplus but withhold our wealth. We cannot afford to be seen in the right places, say the right things, pray fervently, but not let go of what we feel entitled to. And we cannot afford not to learn from our sisters and brothers who have for years borne the brunt of our inequality.

Let's not make a show – let's make a change.

Prayer

May change ring out, not hollow words.
Amen.

Question

Unpack entitlement. Privilege is not something we are 'lucky to have'. More often, it is power, resource or influence taken from others. Where do you see this in yourself or in our systems? This can be a group discussion or a personal reflection.

Action

Inform yourself and share. Ahead of COP26, look up your country's specific commitments – its NDC (Nationally Determined Contribution) – and lobby for those commitments to be honoured:

www4.unfccc.int/sites/NDCStaging/Pages/All.aspx

Sally Foster-Fulton

Sally Foster-Fulton is Christian Aid's Head of Nations and Church Relations. She is an ordained minister in the Church of Scotland, former Convener of the Kirk's Church and Society Council and an associate member of the Iona Community. Sally is married to Stuart and they have two fabulous daughters, Alex and Gracie.

25th Sunday after Pentecost (B)

Reading

When he was sitting on the Mount of Olives opposite the temple, Peter, James, John, and Andrew asked him privately, 'Tell us, when will this be, and what will be the sign that all these things are about to be accomplished?' Then Jesus began to say to them, 'Beware that no one leads you astray. Many will come in my name and say, "I am he!" and they will lead many astray. When you hear of wars and rumours of wars, do not be alarmed; this must take place, but the end is still to come.'

(Mark 13:3–7, NRSV)

Reflection

What we call 'apocalyptic' *'seizes hold of a memory as it flashes up at a moment of danger',*[1] as Walter Benjamin said. We find it in Daniel, written during the persecution of Antiochus IV Epiphanes (reigned 175–164 BC), and in Revelation, probably written during the persecution of Domitian, and we find it in Mark 13. This passage may well derive from the final period of the struggle for Jerusalem in AD 69–70 but it has spoken to Christians through the ages, as it does to us today in our moment of danger, calling to mind the memory of G-d's presence and promise.

Revelation speaks of four horsemen who bring death and destruction (Rev 6:1–6). Today we know these as overpopulation, loss of biodiversity, resource depletion and climate change. Taken together these could lead to civilisational collapse and even the end of human life on earth.

Apocalypse, however, was never written for the thrill of terrifying its readers or to provoke despair. On the contrary, it was written to stiffen resistance, to remind its readers that G-d reigns, to affirm the purposes of the G-d of life. All apocalypse trades in symbols and codes, like all resistance movements to the present day (see Extinction Rebellion).

Jesus is seated on the Mount of Olives. Mark's readers remember: this is the place from which YHWH will go forth to fight the enemies of Jerusalem (Zech 14:2–4).

The disciples (i.e., you and me) ask for a sign. We have forgotten. 'The Pharisees came and began to argue with him, asking him for a sign from heaven, to test him. And he sighed deeply in his spirit and said … 'Truly I tell you, no sign will be given to this generation' (Mark 8:11–12). Instead we must stay alert ('*blepete*': Mark 13:5, 9, 23, 33). See that no one leads you astray: everywhere there is misinformation, the kingdom of lies. Do not be alarmed! But do practise discernment and make sure you are not deceived (Mark 13:22).

But surely, Jesus, there's more than enough reason to be alarmed! Yes, but panic helps no one. '*The end is not yet.*' Instead of panic the call to discipleship is reaffirmed – this is what Mark means by sending us back to 'Galilee' at the end of the gospel. What does this mean? Jesus has told us repeatedly: witness, casting out demons (Mark 6:7), forming a movement (3:14), service (10:43).

Our witness is to the G-d who creates all things out of love and joy, who loves the created order infinitely, who wants us to understand it as gift, and therefore to cry out at the careless destruction of this gift as the most horrid blasphemy.

The demons we have to cast out are the demons of aggressive appropriation, of money as a false idol, of military power as the answer to all our problems, of contempt and hatred for any group we do not belong to. This exorcism is often through symbolic actions which we call liturgies: protesting before government departments, at nuclear bases, and at destructive developments like new coal mines.

The movement is called in the New Testament '*ekklesia*', the word for the citizen assembly in Athens, used to translate '*quahal*', the assembly of the tribes to decide on defensive action – in this case, action in defence of the threatened earth.

And service, because the revolution we are called to is a revolution of love, not hate, so that our resistance is based on compassion, love of our neighbour and of our enemy, and of the earth, which is gifted to us. Our resistance is rooted in the love of G-d. As Francis put it:

Most High, all-powerful, good Lord,
Yours are the praises, the glory, the honour, and all blessing.
To You alone, Most High, do they belong,
and no man is worthy to mention Your name.
Be praised, my Lord, through all your creatures …
Praised be You, my Lord, through Sister Mother Earth,
who sustains us and governs us and who produces
varied fruits with coloured flowers and herbs.

Action

UK: Ask every member of the congregation to send a postcard to the local council asking if it has passed a motion to endorse the Climate and Ecological Emergency Bill (www.ceebill.uk) and if they communicated this motion to their Members of Parliament.

Elsewhere: Find out what legislation is being prepared in your country to combat climate and ecological emergency, and advocate for its support.

Tim Gorringe

Tim Gorringe is a retired teacher of theology, non-retired minister and full-time smallholder. He lives on the edge of Dartmoor with his wife Gill, 40 sheep, 26,000 bees, two cockerels and 15 chickens. He is a member of the Iona Community.

Note

1. From Thesis on the Philosophy of History, Walter Benjamin, 1940

Last Sunday of the Year: Reign of Christ (B)

Reading

Then Pilate entered the headquarters again, summoned Jesus, and asked him, 'Are you the King of the Jews?' Jesus answered, 'Do you ask this on your own, or did others tell you about me?' Pilate replied, 'I am not a Jew, am I? Your own nation and the chief priests have handed you over to me. What have you done? Jesus answered, 'My kingdom is not from this world. If my kingdom were from this world, my followers would be fighting to keep me from being handed over to the Jews. But as it is, my kingdom is not from here.' Pilate asked him, 'So you are a king?' Jesus answered, 'You say that I am a king. For this I was born, and for this I came into the world, to testify to the truth. Everyone who belongs to the truth listens to my voice.'

(John 18:33–37)

Reflection

John's Gospel has a strange – and unjustified – reputation of being iffy about Creation. A pretext for detachment from justice and environmental issues.

But to which 'world' is Christ's 'kingdom' not subject?

Strange, because John's Gospel so forcefully affirms the incarnation of Christ in the Earth. The Word is made (inclusive) flesh, rather than merely human or 'man', though the very specific vocabulary for such narrowing of scope was freely available. That makes biblical sense. The rainbow covenant is between God and 'all flesh'. More couple than threesome.

One excuse for this impression is John's multi-layered use of 'world' to mean both the 'very-human world' (in which Pilate is immersed, preoccupied, baffled) and the Whole Earth – specifically as we experience it.

Unlike Humpty Dumpty, I doubt the aspiration on the writer's part absolutely to restrict meaning to context. 'Neither more nor less.'[1]

Is the 'world' that *'God so loves that God's child is given, that those who trust should not be lost, but find the life they need to see them through this age'* (John 3:16), the same 'world' Christ's kingdom evades?

Hardly. Jesus is the opposite of alien! God is surely more 'at home' here than we are. But if your own 'whole world' is narrow, detached human interest, disregarding your dependence on fellow creatures you despise and disregard, then Christ's scope is so much wider.

Or even if you don't despise them – even if you love to be refreshed by resort to nature – the toxic mental detachment from Creation we've inherited, encourages the complacency of 'nature can look after itself'. What sort of 'truth' can we afford to belong to, and expect to survive?

The 'world' whose laws *'never should be broken'* (Ps 148) is now trampled flagrantly on an industrial global scale, though with ironic humility, humanity never imagined we could so comprehensively disrupt climate or exhaust 'resources'.

To act in such a way that the Goldilocks window of balanced climate, which has cradled all our history, is shattered, amounts to cosmic rebellion. What does it take to recognise ourselves as enemies of the 'world'?

A modern view of the outer reaches of the universe is a luxury resource for awe and wonder, and in time of emergency, this tempts with too much scope for skywards gawping, like the disciples at the Ascension, before they were brought rudely down to Earth by – of all beings – the (heavenly) angels!

We're not well-served, either, by science fiction's preoccupation with other dimensions messing around with our thoughts. For the purposes of our life, the living Earth entire, but also alone, is a sufficient experience of God's Beloved World, for whom that other Beloved is offered. Look close enough down to Earth, and every wonder-hunger is satisfied without evading urgency. We don't even yet know of creatures on which our life depends.

It's bizarre, but even a delightful preoccupation with faith/science dialogue can assist in the evasion of climate issues. 'Isn't God wonderful who made the universe? – we can deal with the mundane emergencies some other time.' The mainstream theology I was trained in – a spirituality in academic clothing – likewise seems to operate on the assumption that nothing dangerous or decisive is about to occur, just so long as we're taking an Ent-long[2] time to ponder it.

But the urgency of change is a transformative context in every use of sacred story. As the church year ends we should ponder which world we want to live in. Which world might yet be sustained. And how.

Friends of Jesus, partnered with life

Tune: Walton or Fulda

King now, we call you, Lord, and more;
though from our dawn, you delegate:
a servant Christ, Creation's friend,
a wind that blows as sails unfurl.

Can we command the wind and waves?
Can we make just injustice raw?
Can we exploit and know no end?
Alas, we've tried: a wounded world!

We need your help – this much is clear!
And wisdom to use every gift.
And listening to Creation's voice.
And love, to bring fresh Good News home!

Question

Is there a part of Christian scripture or tradition which you believe is at odds with urgent care for Creation, or that you have heard used to justify denial or evasion of environmental action? Where does truth lie in this?

Action: One beautiful thing

The human population is around 8 billion. Doing, yourself, every possible environmentally friendly thing you can find on the Internet will not make a – measurable – difference, though it might wear you out. Instead, do one beautiful thing, which sustains you in your ongoing commitment to care of Creation, and gives hope to one other person. And whatever form this takes, think of it as a prayer: leave it to God to measure the impact.

David J.M. Coleman

Iona Community member David J.M. Coleman is a URC minister/digital artist, currently Environmental Chaplain for Eco-Congregation Scotland (Scotland's happiest apocalyptic preacher!) encouraging local churches and those involved in the training of Christian leaders to discover the genuine green thread that runs through the best of faith and tradition. He is a widower, with two adult children.

Notes

1. 'When I use a word,' Humpty Dumpty said, in rather a scornful tone, 'it means just what I choose it to mean – neither more nor less.' (*Through the Looking Glass*, Lewis Carroll)

2 'You must understand, young Hobbit, it takes a long time to say anything in Old Entish. And we never say anything unless it is worth taking a long time to say.' (*The Two Towers*, J.R.R. Tolkien)

Sources and acknowledgements

Essays

Introduction

In addition to our response to the teachings of scripture about creation, we must always be attuned to place and to praxis. So we asked Iona Community folk from very different parts of the world – from Fairhope, Alabama to Frankfurt, Germany; from Glasgow, Scotland to Newcastle, Australia – to add their voices here: describing the impact that climate change is having on the place in which they live, the area of work/activism they are involved in – campaigning, grassroots organising, writing – and their own personal motivation behind their work. By encouraging folk to reflect from their own geography and context, we hoped we could show how climate change affects us all – wherever in the world we are.

As Marksen Masinde and Fridah Wafula from Eldoret, Kenya write:

> *'It is not just about how well we live here, but how well everybody lives everywhere. Changing the narrative of climate change is not a one-man job; it is not for the chosen few. It is the choice everyone needs to make.'*

So here are some essays about some of the choices folk around the world are making; action rooted in scripture and prayer, and in the challenge and support of a worldwide community of hope.

Katharine M. Preston

Drookit!

It's raining. Again. And it's blowing a gale. But it *is* Glasgow, so that's hardly surprising. We're brought up to take comedian Billy Connolly's observation that 'there's no such thing as bad weather – only the wrong clothes', not as humour, but as a practical pointer. But it's raining. Again. Drookit!

As a child in the 1980s, I remember playing football and tennis in the park on red ash – a surface that not only hurt you badly should you fall on it, but flooded easily, rendering play impossible – or grass, which was equally liable to puddle (a common verb in these parts). By the time I was playing football at university in the early 2000s, there was AstroTurf, or 'all-weather surfaces', on which to train and play. There was no need for games to be off. But fast-forward 20 years to today and ask me how many times the 'all-weather' tennis courts that my son and I play on have flooded? Surfaces designed to cope with 'any weather' – absolutely saturated. Again. And once more, the game is off. And I haven't even mentioned the wind.

First World problems, but undeniably a sign of a changed climate. Working for Christian Aid, I've had the opportunity to see the impact that climate change has had on people around the world. Communities that rely on the land for their livelihood are particularly susceptible to erratic and extreme weather, as crops fail due to lack of rain, or flash flooding, or a combination of both. In Ethiopia, communities have watched successive harvests fail due to prolonged periods of drought, followed by flooding. Hot, wet weather then leads to perfect conditions for desert locusts, which destroy crops that had been viable. In Asia and South America, drought, high temperatures and periods of flooding have culminated in people being pushed to the brink as their crops fail. In an attempt to get us to take climate change seriously, the failure of coffee and cocoa crops has been well-documented.

My role within Christian Aid enables me to get out and speak to churches and groups about the impact climate change is having, and point people towards actions they can take, both personally and politically, to bring about the change that is needed so that we can properly care for God's creation. One of the most gratifying things is seeing people have that 'lightbulb moment' – when they realise just how climate change is impacting on people and planet, and seeing them all fired up to do something about it. For me, as for so many others, our children and grandchildren are our motivation, as are our sisters and brothers around the world who are already at the sharp end of climate change. Political action is key to solving this, which is why we must demand our leaders be ambitious in reaching legally binding carbon targets.

Climate justice is one of these great justice issues that really forces both global systemic change and individual behavioural change. The lifestyles we have here in 21st century Scotland are designed to be carbon-heavy, with the disposable option usually the easier one. I find it a constant challenge. On one hand it's easy to feel virtuous – we have solar panels; we have an electric car; we use bikes day-to-day; we largely have second-hand furniture and clothes; we're 80% vegan; and we take a packed lunch, water bottle and flask with us wherever we go. We're doing our bit. But we consume more than our fair share. Plastic-wrapped fruit and veg, travel around Scotland to experience the great outdoors, or abroad for some cheap summer sun, or to sports events – all has a carbon footprint.

I believe change is possible. Our history shows us that people coming together for the common good can, and will, prevail. I mentioned the rain, but what about the wind? It has its downside, of course, but it also ensures that Scotland is able to produce a considerable amount of renewable energy from that power we have in abundance. The pandemic has given us the chance to pause the 'norm', and now the focus really needs to be on a just and green recovery that leaves no one behind. A future where God's people and God's planet are able to thrive.

Val Brown

Val Brown, an associate member of the Iona Community, has worked for Christian Aid for nearly 17 years, first as a youth worker and now as Community Relations and Fundraising Manager. Val lives in Glasgow with her husband and two children (14 and 11), and loves sports, gardening and cooking.

Just food for all

I have long been passionate about food justice. From working in rural South Africa, Rwanda and Mali, as well as in Asia, sometimes with the UN, I learned that structural inequality and poverty cause malnutrition, that governments have serious responsibilities, and that good food for all is key to human and social flourishing. Now I fear that climate chaos will worsen the hard conditions many face, because of its impact on farming and food systems, and because of policies proposed to mitigate these effects.

Food is central to human relationships and for health and wholeness. Food is more than nutrients; it's how you show people you care for and respect them, and it's a sign of identity: 'this is us – we are people who grow/cook/eat like this'. And food is essential to many livelihoods, whether growing, processing, shipping, retailing or cooking. Injustice is rife in the food system, from producer to eater, despite Fairtrade and local initiatives. Even in the rich UK many can't afford to eat decently; many farmers and food workers barely earn a living.

How does climate chaos make this worse?

Partly it's because the global food system is already under profound crisis, with loss of biodiversity, pollinators, good soils, clean water and young labour. These challenges are being made worse by deeply unstable global weather systems as a result of climate change. The worst-hit regions are the world's breadbaskets; key transport routes are also threatened. Conflict over diminishing resources (especially water and land) and migration will increase, made worse by vulnerabilities the pandemic has exacerbated. UK food security is affected too: we import half our food needs, so are susceptible to volatile environments and geopolitical instabilities. Our UK farmers struggle with increasing floods, frosts, pests and droughts.

In turn, as most of us now realise, the global food system itself is having profound effects on climate breakdown, contributing nearly a third of total greenhouse gases. Some is down to food lost or wasted along the supply chain (in transport, processing and in the home); some is through global deforestation, which reduces the planet's ability to capture carbon, much of which comes through conventional agriculture.

What's being done? Much effort is going into 'big tech' solutions, which are increasingly owned by large corporations who don't have the interests of the poor or the soil at heart. What gives me hope is that many small producers, here and around the world, are returning to agro-ecological ways of farming, which work with the natural world to promote practices that mitigate climate change, and which put farmers and communities in the driving seat. Even in the UK there's a shift to new ways of farming and rearing animals, ways which are low or zero greenhouse gas emitting.

We have important roles, too, as food citizens. Many are growing or trying to eat differently: we know we need to eat a largely plant-based diet, preferably from raw, fresh ingredients, so we avoid ultra-processed, industrialised food, however tempting and cheap. (It's only cheap because other people and environments are paying the full cost.) Do we have to cut all meat and dairy to meet carbon targets? Not necessarily – but we should eat much less meat than we currently do. Meat should come from sustainable systems, where grassland ruminant livestock contribute to soil well-being, through transforming nitrogen into organic fertiliser. Eating like this is hard for those with little money; it's a challenge for campaigning groups and policymakers to generate creative policies to ensure food justice can thrive under climate chaos. Unfortunately, the cheapest foods tend to have the worst carbon footprints and costly health outcomes.

Maybe we can begin with refocusing on our kitchens, as Dee Woods of Granville Community Kitchen says, as places of *'repair, resilience, resistance and safety'*[1] – where we rebuild awareness of food sources, creativity and solidarity. We can revalue food in our social, economic and spiritual lives, as that which centres all of us, whatever our income, skills or age, in sustainable living which strengthens the planet.

Elizabeth Dowler

Elizabeth Dowler works on food justice, as a researcher, teacher, writer and activist in food and nutrition, often addressing inequalities. Now retired, she lives in Oxford, and is a member of the Food Ethics Council and of the Iona Community.

Note

1. See https://www.resurgence.org/magazine/article5661-nourishing-the-community.html

Pilgrimage2Paris

All my life I have held a loathing of strenuous exercise. In my schooldays, I would pray for rain so that I'd be spared the humiliation of the tennis court or lacrosse pitch; and in adulthood I would never choose the energetic option. But the concept of going on a pilgrimage was something different. Each year I've stayed on Iona I have walked the island pilgrimage, and most years I have been left with some thing – a conversation, a sight, the words of a reading or a song – that has proved significant as I have reflected afterwards.

More recently I used a 'Columba's Bay moment' to leave behind my fearful self, and that led to my signing up to walk the Pilgrimage2Paris for the Climate Change Summit in November 2015.

Over the years my concern for the future of our beautiful planet has grown, as I have recognised the wounds we inflict on it through our unquestioning habits of consumerism and have heard of the suffering of people all over the world as a result of climate change. My association with the Iona Community has played a big part in this process – as has my role as a volunteer preacher for Christian Aid. A couple of years ago I heard a climate activist from the Philippines speak of the way that climate change is affecting his country, and just last month we heard of five islands that have simply disappeared. So, learning that the Church of England (in which I am a licensed reader/lay minister), CAFOD [Catholic Agency for Overseas Development], Tear Fund and Christian Aid were together organising a pilgrimage from London to Paris to coincide with the start of the 21st session of the Conference of the Parties (COP21) Climate Change Talks, I felt I had to respond. This was partly as a challenge to myself, but equally to show my commitment to the cause and to try to move the hearts of those participating in the talks to reach an agreement.

I won't pretend it wasn't hard. Especially it was hard on the feet ... but no harder on my feet than anyone else's. We encouraged one another and somehow kept going. When I felt tempted to weaken, I felt in my pocket and there was my green Columba's Bay stone, reminding me not to be fearful. Attached to my trusty walking pole was a ribbon saying 'Live, Laugh, Love', which would make me smile through the pain.

Most importantly, what kept me going was the strength provided by people's prayers; we would pray together each morning and most of us prayed silently throughout the day, but I also received text messages from friends telling me that we had been prayed for back home – and that made an enormous difference.

It was liberating to travel light and have all our needs provided for, and to have the time to reflect on how I could simplify my lifestyle. As one who usually dithers in front of the wardrobe each morning, it was marvellous to have the element of choice removed, as we wore the same clothes day after day!

Reaching Paris, we found a city in grief but defiant. Two weeks after the terrorist attacks, security was tight. Open-air gatherings were cancelled and security forces were everywhere. But we did meet with fellow pilgrims and heard some astonishing stories: one couple had cycled 16,000 miles from Vietnam's Mekong Delta. Their tales ensured that we retained an appropriate modesty about our own efforts.

We saw Christiana Figueres receive the petition of support – 1.8 million signatures – and the tears flowed as she thanked us for every single step which, combined, would stretch seven times round the world. And, as you know, the hearts of the world leaders were moved to reach an agreement, which is why we were walking in the first place.

Our journey was hard and it rained almost every day. But despite times of discomfort, I wouldn't have missed it. It was a real time of blessing, in so many ways, and that is my dominant memory. Together we were blessed that we all stayed healthy. We were so blessed by those we met on the way, by the prayers and encouragement of those back home, helping to carry us through, and by the relationships we built with fellow pilgrims. I've changed because I put my life on hold for two and a half weeks to do God's work. It wasn't much, but it was what I could offer. And that change in myself is a huge blessing that will be with me for life. And the best response to climate change is to stand up to it together: every single step we take can make a difference.[1]

Diana Hill

Diana Hill is an associate member of the Iona Community and a Reader in the Church of England. She is a volunteer preacher for Christian Aid and lives in Lichfield with her husband, Peter Phillips.

Note

1. This essay was edited by Kathy Galloway from a longer piece in *Standing on Our Stories: The Justice, Peace and Wholeness Commitment of the Iona Community*, Narrator: Susan Dale, Wild Goose Publications, 2020. First published in *Coracle*, the magazine of the Iona Community.

God made the earth ... then man happened

God creates a self-sustaining environment of people, animals, plants, bodies of water and land. He hands it over to man, whose main role is to manage it. The expected result from this is a balanced ecosystem for generations to come. The environment, however, tells a different story of just how well, or should we say poorly, man has done his part.

In Kenya, one major impact of climate change has been on the weather patterns, most visibly, the rising temperatures and declining rainfall in the main rainy season. The combination of these two elements results in prolonged dry seasons that cause frequent and widespread droughts in the country. Areas that used to receive decent amounts of rain are now receiving little or no rain at all. The effects of these elements on the environment are causing adverse consequences in many other areas.

First is the economy. The yield from staple farming is declining significantly, which affects the economy in multiple ways. Farmers no longer produce surplus food for sale as they used to, which has a double effect on the country. One, farmers no longer have additional resources to afford provisions such as education and medical care. The other is that the general food supply in the country is less than the demand from the growing population. This has forced the government to import basic food. Some farmers have completely lost their land to the growing desert encroaching on what was previously arable land.

In addition, climate change has significantly affected the cultures of several communities across the country, such as pastoralists, who in years past used to move from place to place in search of pasture for their livestock. They had particular nomadic routes that allowed the pasture enough time to grow while they were away. Now they find themselves having to settle down in one place, buy expensive animal feed, reduce the size of their herds, and in some cases change their way of life completely. Those who have kept up the nomadic life have to stay away from their homes for longer, leaving their families behind for longer periods. The most recent development has seen livestock such as cows, goats and sheep traversing the streets of the cities and town centres in search of any and all greenery.

The most perilous effect so far has been the conflict between wild animals and humans. Forested areas are equally declining, which in turn has reduced the space in which human beings can safely stay out of the way of wild animals. Recently we have had increasing cases of wild animals that have harmed and killed people and domestic animals in their search for food and water. Lions and leopards have gotten into homesteads to prey on goats and sheep. Elephants and hippos have been known to stray onto people's land, destroying the crops in their path.

Recurring droughts and floods have posed a challenge to both human and animal life. While floods have people and animals drowning to death or being buried alive in mudslides, droughts have in some cases seen the same communities starving to death. The rapid and about-turn changes in the weather have caught many off guard and unprepared.

The sad truth is that we should have already learnt from previous experience about the effects of our small individual actions on the entire globe. But a big percentage of our population is still ignorant about it. It is not just about how well we live here, but how well everybody lives everywhere. Changing the narrative of climate change is not a one-man job; it is not for the chosen few. It is the choice everyone needs to make.

Marksen Masinde and Fridah Wafula

Marksen Masinde and Fridah Wafula are a couple, father and mother from Kenya. Fridah is an associate member of the Iona Community as well as the founder of the Saidiana Women Project (www.saidianawomenproject.org). Marksen is a friend of the Community and a retired Church minister working diversely with communities in Kenya.

Living lightly at Camas

Camas is the Iona Community's Outdoor Activity Centre on the Hebridean island of Mull, which is part of a chain of islands rich in history, culture, geology and ecology. Islands around the world have faced devastation due to the climate crisis and the risks for the Hebrides are very real – rising sea levels and dramatic weather changes are already causing increased coastal erosion and affecting the land and the way of life.

Camas has long embodied a vision to live simply and lightly in harmony with the earth, and to be both a practical and educational example of sustainability. Being in tune with the cycle of the seasons, the rhythms of the earth, the wildlife and the elements is both a way of life and a necessity in a place that is a mile and a half down a boggy track, which relies on the wind and sun for power and where supplies can only be brought in by boat or wheelbarrow!

Over the years Camas staff have expressed and evolved this mission through minimising waste, growing their own fruit and vegetables in an ever-expanding organic garden and through planting trees. In 2018 a large new native woodland was created with help from guests, generous financial donations and trees from the Woodland Trust. This is a living symbol for both the present and the future.

The integrated Camas programme supports young people and adults to engage with the environment through activities including kayaking, gardening, foraging, walks, reflection, camping, conservation, campfires and creative arts. All guests take an active role in the common life of the community through practical tasks such as harvesting veg from the garden, helping with the cooking, taking out the compost, cleaning the compost toilets. For guests, many of whom come from an urban environment, being in a wild place can be a powerful and challenging experience. As former Leader of the Iona Community Kathy Galloway writes: '... *the work at Camas is so important – it offers an alternative vision of community, ecology and sustainability to young people whose experience of those things is often entirely absent or destructive*'.[1]

In *Down the Track: A Camas Anthology* (Wild Goose Publications, 2021), young people and adults reflect on their experience of connecting with the earth in comments such as these:

'I will care for the earth more, recycle things and use less plastic.'

Young person

'The best part of the week was when we dug up potatoes from the garden. I have never done that before and didn't like the worms, but we all worked together as a team and made chips for our tea.'

Young person

'We helped out pulling bracken to make room for the trees. My arms and legs were aching but it was brilliant to know we were a tiny part of helping to regenerate this area.'

Group Leader[2]

As for many staff, Camas was influential for me when I worked there as a young volunteer, then as Camas Coordinator, over twenty years ago. As a youth worker coming from a working-class town, I learnt a lot which led me to a deeper relationship with the earth. This informed my subsequent work, activism, interests and creativity, some of which has included planting over 2000 trees, setting up community gardens and allotments, taking vulnerable young people on bothy trips in the Highlands, supporting others as they learn to forage and grow their own food, helping to develop a social enterprise that sells natural cosmetics, using recycled and donated materials in crafts and craftivism. More recently I was a member of the Camas Committee for seven years, and it was a privilege to feel I could give something back to a place that has given me much.

Camas is a microcosm where seeds are planted and hearts touched. George MacLeod referred to Iona as a *'sending place'*, and the same is true of Camas: it sends us out with the challenge to *'live simply so that others may simply live'*.

Rachel McCann

Rachel McCann is a former social worker who retrained in gardening; she currently uses those skills in local community projects in the south of Scotland. Rachel is an associate member of the Iona Community and the editor of Down the Track: A Camas Anthology, *which will be published by Wild Goose later in 2021.*

Notes

1. From *Living by the Rule: the Rule of the Iona Community*, Kathy Galloway, Wild Goose Publications, 2010

2. From *Down the Track: A Camas Anthology*, Rachel McCann (Ed.), to be published by Wild Goose in 2021

Camas Outdoor Activity Centre,
Ardfenaig,
Bunessan,
Isle of Mull,
Scotland, UK
PA67 6DX

www.iona.org.uk
camas@iona.org.uk

To see a wonderful short film about Camas:

https://www.youtube.com/watch?v=93PQO3z8zis

Rising through the third great flood

I grew up in the village of Leurbost on the Isle of Lewis in a parish called North Lochs. Water, both salt and fresh, and in the air both vertically and horizontally, was sovereign in our world. In the past, neither roads nor fibre cables, but the ocean was our forebears' superhighway.

So it is that a necklace drapes around much of the coast, the jewels of which are sacred sites in nature, the Gaelic names of which mark out a plethora of bygone oratories, convents, monasteries, holy wells – and the *teampaill* or 'temples', as the old churches are known. Abandoned though these were with the Protestant Reformation of 1560, as R.S. Thomas put it in a Welsh context: *'The parish/has a saint's name time cannot/unfrock.'*[1]

The connections to the Celtic saints are everywhere. When growing up, we'd hear how the dead in olden days were taken round by boat for burial at *Teampall Chaluim Chille* on Saint Columba's Island. Eat your heart out, Iona. It's one thing to have an abbey. But a 'temple'!

It's an amazing thing to make a pilgrimage – I beg your pardon, an outing of historical interest – to these sites with local people. I've heard the Gaelic Psalms sung out at *Chaluim Chille* – literally, Columba of the Church – and this is worship hauntingly evocative.

Evocative of what? Well might you ask. Evocative of God. 'O taste and see', and these days, though I'm Quaker by convincement, there are times when the Presbyterian catechism of 1647 as we learned it by rote just nails the point: *'There is but ONE ONLY, the living and true God.'*

Nine miles to the north-east, near Stornoway, is another church and major cemetery with the same dedication. But *Eaglais Chaluim Chille* is being eaten round the edges by the sea. The council and a community trust have built up sea defences. They'll last a generation. But with climate change, the oceans of the world are rising by an inch in every seven years, and speeding up. In our north-east Atlantic storms, the peaks of waves are higher than before. The sea takes back her own, and yet, there is a sadness in her sough. A friend, a priest in Ireland's Aran Isles, was on the phone the other day. He asked me what of activism as the UN prepares to bring its climate conference, COP26, to Glasgow where I live now. In many ways, my books distil my activism. I told him of a dream I'd had recur while writing. It's as if, I said, we've mostly started at the splashy, shouty end of the pool. But we need to deepen in our activism. Wade out, and learn to swim, and then to dive down at the deep end: and even, how to breathe underwater.

He said the Celtic hermits didn't try to change the world. They changed themselves. They went out to be alone with God and nature. And then the world changed round them. That's faith, and prayer in action, *peregrini*.

Rarely I repeat a story, but such is its importance that my last two books retold the Hebridean legend of the three great floods.

The first was that of the Creation. The second, that of Noah, born of human violence. But the third great flood, the bards say, has yet to come. In 1869 an old woman told the chronicler of the *Carmina Gadelica* that there will be *'an overflowing of the Atlantic'*. A time will come to pass when *'the walls of the churches shall be the fishing-rocks of the people'*. And there, amongst these temple ruins, *'the pale-faced mermaid, the marled seal and the brown otter shall race and run and leap and gambol – like the children of men at play'*.

One version tells how the isles themselves will be submerged, except Iona. It will rise up on the waters, *'and float there like a crown'*.

I ask you, what qualities of spirit might breathe underwater, and rise up like a crown? What activism might faith groups bring? I can but think of Saint Columba's dying words:. *'Love one another unfeignedly. Peace.'*

Alastair McIntosh

Alastair McIntosh's most recent book, Riders on the Storm: The Climate Crisis and the Survival of Being *(Birlinn), is described by the world's most prominent climate scientist, Michael Mann, as 'a life-giving vision for our collective future'. His previous book,* Poacher's Pilgrimage, *recounts a 12-day Hebridean walk, an ecology of the imagination, that opens to a Christian vision for the third millennium. Alastair is an associate member of the Iona Community.*

Note

1. From 'The moon in Lleyn', by R.S. Thomas

Dicing with tipping points

'Fish don't know they are surrounded by water,' my contemplatively inclined friend said. 'Hmm, I know when I am,' I replied. Although I liked that analogy for the unseen, all-embracing presence of God, in 1986 I was a novice kayaker, inadvertently entertaining companions by capsizing on every club trip. However flat the water, there was always a moment of surprise when my incompetence was suddenly overcome by the laws of physics and I was flipped to be eye to eye with the fishes. With effort over a long while, I learnt how to recover balance at the tipping point, and then how to enjoy relaxed equilibrium, feeling at one with the water even in turbulence.

A wind-enforced pause on Iona, during a holiday kayaking around Mull, led to me meeting the Iona Community in 1989. I heard about Camas, and next year was resident there for the summer, on leave from my job in London. Preparing for this, I was excited by Steve Van Matre's approaches to outdoor experience. He prioritised connecting to the earth with each of the senses. For example, by finding a randomly chosen colour of the rainbow in the plants and rocks; with fingertips, exploring the bark of a tree as if walking a new land. His approach resonated with my experience: encounter creation, come to love and feel connected to the earth. Study and understanding might come later, but the cherishing and connection are much more vital. So, when I came to spend the season at Camas it was with delight in the opportunity to share such experiences.

In 1992 I moved to Edinburgh to be closer to the sea and mountains and to be able to discern my next steps. My new day job was writing computer software to support environmental research. Decades ago, it was clear that human activity, by ignoring the laws of physics, risked reaching tipping points that would cause major disruption of the climate and ecosystems. What was missing, outside the Iona Community, was a way to touch hearts and minds, so human activity would change: poets, artists and liturgists were needed. Where was the regular Sunday liturgy connecting to the cosmic story of grace over 14 billion years? Why was not *all* water deemed 'holy'?!

In 2015 Pope Francis assimilated evidence and expertise from around the world, and insight from past Church teaching, and published the beautiful document *Laudato Si'*. This presented the science, reflected on the causes of the ecological crises, and called the world to conversion personally, in community life and sociopolitically. His foundation was also to cherish the earth of which we are a part – cherish rather than exploit and abuse, which has led to the present cry of the earth and of the poor. In Roman Catholic life we are still catching up with Pope Francis even after six years.

This year we don't commune together in the Eucharist, but through lockdown for the common good. I work from home with computer models of the climate and, in the evenings, seek to promote two causes. The first is that our communion with the earth and all humanity must include the Palestinians. There is a tipping point here too, but it's by design not accident, to make justice for Palestinians much harder to achieve. The second cause is to absorb and promote the vision of *Laudato Si'* and kindred initiatives like Eco-Congregation Scotland.

As sea level rises and the climate is disrupted, catastrophe is already the experience of so many poorer communities. These are the first tipping points, due to inattention, self-indulgence, apathy and power-seeking in the 'developed' world. There are signs of progress, of movement towards justice for all the earth – yet the risk is so great and the need so urgent! We're in a long struggle and a life-enhancing one: learning to commune in graceful equilibrium at one with all the earth.

Mike Mineter

Mike Mineter was born in Manchester, grew up in Birmingham and now lives in Edinburgh. He became an associate member of the Community in 1993 and a full member in 2013 at Govan Old Church. He convenes the Iona Community's Common Concern Network on Israel/Palestine.

Making a difference

'Many small people, who in many small places do many small things, can alter the face of the world.'

African proverb written on the Berlin Wall

Climate change is no longer a catchword, something that will happen many years from now, but instead we have become witnesses of changes on a much larger scale than expected, even for those of us who have been quite aware of the threat of the human exploitation of the earth and its valuable resources. We witness the ruin of our good soil through conventional agriculture, air pollution through excessive travel by car and plane, the extinction of a huge number of insects and other animals. I still remember, 20 to 30 years ago, driving longer distances through Germany: on arrival at your destination you had to clean your windscreen from all those little bugs you had hit on your ride. I haven't had to do that for many years; they have more or less disappeared.

Over the last years Germany has experienced unusual and more frequent severe windstorms, tornados and flooding. With increasing frequency, we have extremely hot summers, the heat staying for weeks on end, drying out the country and the forests. Today about a third of our forests are lost or at least damaged due to drought and bark beetles and have to be replanted. In Frankfurt, 98% of our city forest is affected.

It is time to change our lifestyles dramatically. In order to live more simply and mindfully, we will have to relearn many things, and refamiliarise ourselves with nature, God's wonderful gift to us. We have become estranged from the natural world around us. How many flowers or animals in the fields and forests can you identify and name? Did you know that even the humble daisy in the meadow, *Bellis perennis*, has healing powers? Its leaf rosettes are delicious in a salad all year around and contain about five times more vital substances than the vegetables we buy in supermarkets.

I am part of a team of leaders of a grassroots network in the Episcopal Church which focuses on creation care and increasing the awareness and commitment of its members to make small changes towards carbon neutrality. That will not be an easy task, as parishioners range from climate-change deniers to climate activists like myself. I started with a call to a special Lent programme, a 'Zero Waste Challenge', discussing all the options to improve our wasteful lifestyle towards a more sustainable way of living, with little tasks for each day. For instance, where is your closest Zero Waste shop or farmers' market or repair café? And in my personal experience of being on this road for several years now, this is not at all about self-denial and sacrifice, but about empowerment, independence and fulfilling happiness. And it is an adventure: at the beginning of the Lent programme you enter a supermarket and see that almost EVERYTHING is wrapped in plastic, and then you can't buy anything wrapped in plastic for the next 40 days. What an eye-opener!

Of course, I don't expect everyone in the parish to achieve zero waste in 40 days. Our motto is the African proverb from the piece of the former Berlin Wall:

> *'Many small people, who in many small places do many small things, can alter the face of the world.'*

Think of the history of Berlin, with the peaceful revolution in 1989. Many small people indeed brought on the peaceful revolution. It still seems to be a miracle, as no one in Germany had anticipated that. And I hope that we will do the same.

After Lent, the programme will continue on a wider range of climate-change-related topics, with monthly talks covering areas like housing, travel, food, living with less, digital waste, eco-investment … The start with a small, dedicated group has been encouraging and we will see where it leads us. There are similar programmes in other denominations in Germany and in neighbourhoods around the country. We keep taking our small steps, and things are changing.

Monica Mueller-Roemer

Monica Mueller-Roemer, a member of the Iona Community in Germany, has a special interest in using wild plants for self-sufficiency and healing and gives various courses to help bring people closer to nature and the environment. Now retired, she was previously an application developer in the airline industry.

The climate crisis and biodiversity loss
Humility and healing on the twofold way

Having fought on the frontlines of biodiversity conservation in tropical forest hotspots for three decades, recently I retired to coastal Alabama on the Northern Gulf of Mexico. Alabama's dark history of racism and poverty was captured by Harper Lee in her classic Southern Gothic novel *To Kill A Mockingbird*. Lee conjured foreboding themes like evil; oppressive poverty; the supernatural. One imagines beautiful live oak and swamp cypress trees draped with ominous Spanish moss and clothed with hopeful resurrection fern.

Indeed, Alabama is blessed with natural beauty – from the Cumberland Plateau mountains in the north to the subtropical Lower Alabama coast, where five great rivers from the highlands entwine to nourish the species-rich Mobile-Tensaw River Delta, a biodiversity hotspot. Alabama ranks among the highest globally for endemic species of fish, turtles, crayfish, mussels, amphibians, oaks, flowers and forest types. The Delta is called 'Alabama's Amazon', and like Amazonia it's under threat from human indifference.

'Biodiversity conservation' protects entire ecosystems and species diversity by empowering local villages. This means seeing humans, animals and plants as integral ecology – an interacting and interdependent ecological assemblage. It requires the hard work of creating nature reserves, defending native people's land-tenure rights, holding extractive industries like timber and mining accountable, developing protection plans for species and sacred groves, organising community-based natural resource management, enhancing human nutrition and rural health. Respect for local cosmology and eco-spirituality is essential.

Typically, I'd engage villages by asking traditional healers, spiritual leaders and hunters to 'Tell me about your people and how they came to be here.' Community empowerment entails yielding space, listening with your heart, nourishing dignity, amplifying voices. Finding common sacred ground. All cultures have taboos and theophanies regarding the interconnectedness of the web-of-life, their inseverable tie to the land. Oglala Sioux Holy Man Black Elk captured this world view when he said everything is One, because all beings pray to the Great Spirit – that if you listen to the breeze in the cottonwood tree, you will hear its prayers. Indigenous people, relying on their wits for survival, are those most impacted by environmental desecration. As any sentient conservationist learns, one must either partner to solve the problems of the rural poor who live daily with wild creatures, or those creatures and their wilderness will perish.

Climate change threatens one-third of all plant and animal species with extinction. It's a threat multiplier, an accelerant poured on every facet of environmental desecration – like diminished microbial communities in the soil essential to agriculture; phenological mismatch where plant food and insects that already stressed animals rely on now come too early or too late; night-sky light pollution that threatens nocturnal and crepuscular creatures adapted to diffused light. The heralds of climate change – hurricanes, droughts, wildfires, global ice loss, new viruses – are the consequences of countless human acts of commission and omission.

Environmentalist Gus Speth wrote that initially he believed the existential issue of global warming would be solved with a few decades of empirical science. As evidence accumulated, he realised that the core problems – selfishness, greed and apathy – cannot be solved by science, because that requires spiritual transformation beyond its purview.[1] Catholic theologian Richard Rohr has claimed the more interconnected we are to the web-of-life, the more saintly we become.[2]

We've abandoned interbeing. Re-enchantment means being in right relations, honouring a covenant. Native peoples and early Christianity have much to teach us. The ninth century Irish theologian John Scotus Eriugena admonished that the light of divine knowledge receded when humankind abandoned God, that Eternal Light is revealed in a twofold way – through scripture and through creatures. He asked us to observe the beauty of all creatures, to feel gratitude towards them and to comprehend them as the Word of God, because God is in All. Today's process theology envisions a similar dynamic.

Modernity has ripped humanity from our root mass. Humans must be repotted into the Whole of Creation – from the soil to the celestial. Wherever our little corner of Paradise shelters us, we can reconnect, re-enchant, protect. Like St Columba, we must fear the sound of the axe.[3] We find healing through humility and intentionality when we listen to and comprehend with our hearts the stories of all persons – human and non-human – who would tell us 'about their people and how they came to be here'.

Richard A. Nisbett

Richard A. Nisbett is a retired university professor and administrator, working at the transdisciplinary interface of anthropology, ecology and public health. He lived and worked among indigenous tropical forest people in Africa, the Circum-Caribbean and South East Asia. His environmental passions include eco-theology, poverty and rural health, biodiversity conservation, community disease ecology, and deforestation. He is an associate member of the Iona Community.

Notes

1. *Shared Planet: Religion and Nature*, BBC Radio 4, 1 October 2013

2. See https://cac.org/the-communion-of-saints-2016-12-14

3. See http://www.orth-transfiguration.org/st-columba-521-597

Close to home

I read an article recently about balsam fir *(Abies balsamea)* and global warming that brought grief to my heart.

Balsams are an elegantly conical, soft-needled, evocatively fragrant tree that prefers the clear, cool air of higher elevations, including the upper slopes of our New York Adirondack Mountains. Around here, they are prized as the best Christmas trees, and are commercially grown for that market. Wildlife finds sustenance in the cones, humans like the lumber for framing and medicinal use of an essential oil from the needles continues from Indigenous times to the present. Because of the lovely fragrance, a traditional gift from these parts includes a cloth pillow stuffed with balsam needles.

I have one of these pillows on my desk now, as I write. I bring it to my nose, and olfactory memories transport me to wilderness, camping and a 'lean-to', the floor of which is traditionally spread with balsam boughs for a soft bedding upon which to throw blankets and sleeping bags for nights out amid the stars and calls of loons.

Because they grow very slowly, balsams are having a particularly hard time with climate change. Climatic conditions are shifting northward up to four miles per year, far faster than this species can migrate, given associated changes in insect pests, infrequent seed dispersal, disease, extreme weather. Balsams may be gone from my world in a matter of a decade or two.

My heart aches at this.

I live in a farmland valley alongside the Adirondack Mountains. Generally warmer temperatures mean we can now take a stab at growing okra or sweet potatoes alongside our peas and carrots. There are occasional floods over the banks of local rivers due to catastrophic storms, and definitely fewer days of snow cover so vital to our winter tourist industry. Ticks carrying the debilitating Lyme disease are multiplying due to the lack of hard, long freezing winter temperatures that used to kill them.

But the climate crisis rarely makes local headlines. At least at this point, fewer lives and livelihoods are directly threatened here, as opposed to low-lying or dry areas of the country where floods and fires dominate the seasonal news cycles. And because we are in a very rural area of the northeast, we are less affected by the forced migration of people from the southern parts of the

Americas because of climate change.

On the other hand, forced migration of other animals and plants as a direct consequence of a changing climate is happening here. It is less noticeable because it occurs more slowly. We read articles or share observations with neighbours, and, over time, become aware of the changes.

The preciousness of a special relationship with a particular species or landscape, in the wild or right near to where we live, may feel very personal, very parochial, almost selfish. Not a matter of concern for a global gathering of experts and politicians trying to save the planet. But if we dismiss the loss of these softly familiar companions inhabiting the world alongside us as less consequential, we risk relegating the climate crisis to other places, other people, affected in other ways, and will be therefore less engaged, less likely to act.

And we must act.

Because the climate crisis rests hardest on those least responsible for it, seeking climate justice must be a primary concern of any community of faith. But they should not forget their traditional pastoral role as healers and accompaniers alongside people who grieve the loss of deeply loved companions close to home, be they species or landscapes.

Although I do show up upon occasion to a march or protest, my activism is mostly this: writing about the climate crisis, hoping to encourage readers to think, study, act. I also accompany my local church congregation as it seeks to become a 'Creation Justice Church' with the United Church of Christ (similar to the Eco-Congregation Scotland process) and I am part of the Iona Community's Common Concern Network, focusing on the environment.

As I hold the balsam-needle-stuffed pillow to my nose, I think of my work as my responsibility to my balsam relatives.

We work in company with one another.

Katharine M. Preston

Katharine M. Preston is an ecumenical lay preacher and writer, concentrating on issues of social justice and climate change. She and her husband, John Bingham, live on a farm in Essex, New York and are active associates of the Iona Community. Katharine is the author of Field with a View: Science and Faith in a Time of Climate Change, *Wild Goose Publications.*

Love and rage

Climate anxiety is crippling. Climate anxiety is motivating. An activist must recognise both.

I was an angry child. Choose whichever adjective you like – spirited, passionate, fiery, stubborn, opinionated – it has been used to describe me. Although it always came from a place of compassion, my love for animals and the environment often resulted in anger directed at those who, I felt, showed no compassion towards creation.

At five, I turned vegetarian, after a rather unforgettable incident involving me yelling 'Murderer!' at the driver of a truck full of lambs. At 12, I abandoned my love of horseriding after feeling that the horses' welfare was not a priority. At 14, I remember crying after talking to my church about the consequences of eating meat and dairy. Crying, not because they hadn't listened, but precisely because they *had* listened but didn't seem as stirred or as furious as I was.

For so many years, my passion manifested in the form of anger and did nothing but cripple me. Not only did it leave me in a state of exhaustion, but also meant I communicated with others in the least effective manner. Even worse, intense waves of frustration and anger would often lead to a complete shutdown of my own activism and care, as a coping mechanism.

Especially for someone who is hoping to go into wildlife conservation, the undeniable presence of climate change can often feel incredibly overwhelming – every day there seems to be less wildlife to even conserve.

As I've grown older, I've learnt how to handle my passion, both a gift and a cross to bear, in order to cope better with climate anxiety – when to take action, and when to breathe through it and centre yourself, accepting you're unable to change the world in a day from your room.

Extinction Rebellion (XR) in particular has been pivotal in helping me maintain a sustainable and healthy climate activism. I first became involved with XR Glasgow over a year ago. One of the things that drew me to it was their focus on 'Regenerative Culture' (Regen) – preventing burnout by meditative and restorative activities – which is core to their success and continuity. Although XR is secular, Regen offers space to bring my individual faith to the centre of my activism – to ground myself and feel a presence, even in the midst of intense actions and tough discussions. I have found myself immensely moved during such regenerative moments – among people of many faiths and none, the intertwined power of our and God's will feels most tangible. It is from these moments that power and strength are drawn to fuel action.

As a young climate activist, I am sometimes asked if I feel any resentment towards older generations for their failure to act. I find this hard to answer, as my hard-won advice is that resentment and anger paralyse you, even though coming from a place of care and compassion.

My dad once said to me that God's love and God's wrath are two sides of the same coin, and that you only experience the wrath when standing against God's love. I see a similar rage in my own activism, but it has taken me years to understand which rage is my own human anger, and which rage comes from a divine love/wrath.

At its best, an activist's rage is an expression of God's wrath against injustice. At its worst, rage instead serves one's own fear and agendas, and is paralysing to both the individual and the coming of God's kingdom. Crucial in distinguishing the difference are moments of Regen – moments of stillness and prayer. They offer a Sabbath: time to refocus and remember that there is hope, if we have faith.

Eve Sharples

Eve Sharples, 20 years old, spent several years of her childhood living on Iona, and traces her love of and fascination with wildlife back to the island. She is currently studying Zoology at the University of Glasgow, and hopes to research wildlife conservation, as well as the intersection of spirituality and ecology. She is a member of the Iona Community's Young Adults Group.

'The black summer'

Global warming has had a devastating effect on Australia. The question is: what part has human activity played in changes to weather patterns – and what role can people of faith have in influencing better outcomes for the planet?

Australia has been described as a land of extremes. In 2019-2020, devastating bushfires raged in South Eastern Australia, preceded by three years of severe drought. A meteorologist explained that as the air around the equator heated up, rain-bearing low-pressure systems were being pushed further south toward Antarctica. As the oceans warmed, the Australian land mass became increasingly dry – exposed to high temperatures, low humidity and low soil moisture. Rainfall came from occasional cyclones plus seasonal northern monsoons, mostly around the coastline.

'The black summer' of 2019-2020 resulted in uncontrollable fire where 46 million acres burned, 3500 homes were destroyed, 34 people died as a direct consequence, with 445 deaths from smoke inhalation. Embers carried by gale-force winds spotted up to five kilometres ahead of the fire front, starting new blazes. Rural communities, farms and livestock were devastated, with crops wiped out.

In January 2020, Canberra experienced the worst air quality index on record, severely endangering human health. Smoke from the summer bushfires reached Antarctica, New Zealand, Argentina and Chile.

The horror for me was not only seeing homes and lives destroyed, but observing three huge blazes between Sydney and the Blue Mountains join up to become a firestorm megafire.

Nearly three billion animals were killed or displaced, and birds 'just dropped from the sky' – causing a major extinction event. In an effort to stay alive, some animals shared wombat tunnels with other species. The loss of habitat and food meant survivors were more vulnerable to predators like foxes and feral cats.

Newcastle, in New South Wales, is the world's largest exporter of thermal coal, which is used for electricity generation, a major source of atmospheric pollution. According to local media, in 2019 a record 164.9 million tonnes of coal was exported.

At one time, living near the river port of Newcastle at the mouth of the Hunter River, our health was affected by three coal loaders just upstream. Daily sweeping of the front porch resulted in a small mound of coal dust. The Hunter Valley supports cattle and dairy farms, vineyards, sheep and horses, yet also has 41 coal mines over an area of 450 square kilometres. Open-cut mining in the Upper Hunter Valley is leaving a landscape described as *'a moonscape'*.

Increased exposure to fine particulate matter associated with open-cut mining has aggravated respiratory disease, with increased hospital admissions. Local ecumenical lobbying and protest prevented the installation of a fourth coal loader.

In 2010, as convener of the Hunter Social Justice committee, I moved a motion at the Synod meeting of the Uniting Church NSW/ACT. It proposed that unless two banks, used by the Uniting Church, refrained from supporting new mining of fossil fuels and instead invested in renewal energy, the church would withdraw its funds. The motion was adopted, and went on to the Assembly, where it was also adopted. And the banks complied!

An application to extend an open-cut mine close to a regional centre, which would disturb valuable soil and alluvial aquifers, was opposed by our committee through the Synod and government planners. Our activities included convening a climate change seminar involving experts, conducting an energy survey and supporting an ecumenical blockade of the harbour to draw attention to coal exports. The extension did not eventuate.

Currently, politicians are seeking ways to use the skills of miners in renewable energy and assist vulnerable communities to adapt. Development of a Hydrogen Technology Cluster has been announced locally. Vast numbers of consumers have installed rooftop solar panels. A major bank stopped lending to the Port of Newcastle after adopting policies that prohibit it from entering new finance deals with customers with significant exposure to fossil fuel.

Within Australia, five coal-fired power stations will become uneconomic by 2025 – due to pressure from investment in renewable energy.

The urgent issue of climate challenge can be addressed and people of faith can speak truth to power.

Helen Weavers

Helen Weavers is an associate member of the Iona Community, who has been a volunteer in Iona, as well as a Council member of the Wellspring Community in Australia (https://wellspring-community.com). In her work life Helen was a secretary, a registered nurse, part of an Intentional Interim Ministry team and a lay preacher. Married to Keith, with three sons and four grandchildren, Helen lives in Newcastle, Australia.

God's Good Earth

A service of worship in preparation
for the COP26 Climate Change conference

Introduction

a) Space & layout

The worship space should be large enough to allow people to sit at a safe distance and, if the optional symbolic action is to be included, to move around.

For this symbolic action, three tables should be placed in different parts of the meeting space, each with a large lit candle and either a globe or a map of the world, beside which is a small basket of votive lights. Above or beside each table, place a sign – at the first table saying 'gratitude'; the next 'regret'; the third 'commitment'.

If the space is flexible, set the rows of chairs in a semicircular formation with one or two aisles, rather than in straight rows facing the front.

b) Leadership

There should be more than one leader. A & C should be located where all can see. B need not be at the front if all the texts are printed. Similarly, the readers can be scattered throughout the gathering, standing in their places to read. However, if the gathering is large and microphones are required, all leaders may have to be located where they can be seen.

Leader A: Welcome (ad lib)
         Opening Responses & Dismissal

Leader B: Prayers and Affirmation

Leader C: Introduction to the time of Reflection
         Introduction to the Response

Readers: Three people to share the readings of the biblical texts
         (Three Biblical Insights), or two people to read as
         Narrator & God (On the Eighth Day).

c) Rehearsal

The whole liturgy should be read through in advance with all leaders and readers involved. This allows for any adjustments to be made, and for leaders to feel confident in what they are doing, especially if any are not used to speaking in public. For the experienced and inexperienced alike, God deserves our best as worship leaders, and rehearsing makes for that worthy offering.

d) Music

If singing is permitted, a choice of hymns should be made in advance and printed along with the liturgy. In 'Three Biblical Insights', the sung response is 'This is God's world' (see Appendix). In 'On the eighth day', any Kyrie would be appropriate. In either instance the music should be rehearsed before worship begins.

Order of worship

Gathering & welcome *(ad lib)*

Opening responses *(standing)*

Leader: Believing that God made and loves the world,
ALL: **we gather.**
Leader: That it may be restored to fulfil God's purposes,
ALL: **we pray.**
Leader: To seek a wisdom deeper than our own,
ALL: **we listen.**
Leader: To honour God who gave us a voice,
ALL: **we worship.**

(A song of praise may be sung.)

Prayer *(seated)*

Leader: God,
         God the Maker,
         maker of colour, sound, texture, movement,
         and the ceaseless beauty in living things,
ALL: **we bless you.**

Leader: God,
         God the Maker,
         maker of granite and mustard seed,
         of grey cloud and starlight,
         of earthquake and heartbeat,
ALL: **we bless you.**

Leader: God,
         God the Maker,
         maker of all that is unseen,
         of all that has been,
         of all that words could never capture,
ALL: **we bless you.**

Leader: God,
            God our Maker,
            we, the children of your love,
            the beneficiaries of your kindness,
            the guardians of your creation, bless you.
ALL: **We bless you for your making,**
         your trusting,
         your loving,
         your never-ending goodness.
         Amen.

REFLECTIONS

Choose either Three biblical insights *(below), or* On the eighth day *(see Appendix).*

Three biblical insights

Leader: Here are three different sets of readings,
            representative of biblical witness,
            which offer a window into the relationship
            between humanity and God's creation.

            Before and after the readings we sing these words:

            This is God's world, given on loan;
            no other earth shall be our home;
            so let us bless, honour and tend
            what God in love created.
            (See Appendix for music)

1. Creation is a source of wonder

Reader 1:   Who supported the sea at its birth,
              when it burst in flood from the womb –
              when I established its bounds,
              set its barred doors in place and said,
              'Thus far shall you come and no further'?

              Have you gone down to the springs of the sea
              or walked in the unfathomable deep?

Have you comprehended
the vast expanse of the world?

Whose womb gave birth to the ice,
and who was the mother of the hoar-frost
which lays a stony cover over the waters? *(From Job 38)*

Reader 2:   Look at the birds in the sky ...
consider the lilies in the field ... *(Matthew 6:26–28)*

Song: This is God's world

2. Creation worships its maker

Reader 3:   The meadows are clothed with sheep
and the valleys decked with grain,
so that with shouts of joy they break into song. *(Psalm 65:13)*

Reader 2:   Let the heavens rejoice and the earth be glad;
let the sea resound and everything in it.
Let the fields exult and all that is in them;
let all the trees of the forest shout for joy
before the Lord. *(Psalm 96:11–12)*

Reader 3:   Praise the Lord from the earth,
you sea monsters and ocean depths ...
all mountains and hills,
all fruit trees and cedars,
wild animals and all cattle,
creeping things and winged birds. *(Psalm 148:7–10)*

Reader 1:   The whole created universe in all its parts
groans as if in the pangs of childbirth. *(Romans 8:22)*

Song: This is God's world

3. Humanity is charged with responsibility

Reader 3: The Lord took the man and put him
in the garden of Eden
to be the guardian and servant of the earth. *(Genesis 2:15)*

Reader 1: For six years you may sow your fields
and prune your vineyards and gather the harvest,
but in the seventh year
the land is to have a sabbatical rest,
a sabbath to the Lord.

No land may be sold outright,
because the land is mine,
and you come to it as aliens and tenants of mine.
(Leviticus 25:3–4 & 23)

Reader 3:   Your wrongdoing has upset nature's order,
and your sins have kept away her bounty. *(Jeremiah 5:25)*

Reader 1: The earth lurches like a drunkard;
the sins of its inhabitants weigh heavy on it,
and it falls, to rise no more. *(Isaiah 24:20)*

Reader 2: The wages you never paid to the men
who mowed your fields are crying aloud against you,
and the outcry of the reapers has reached
the ears of the Lord of Hosts. *(James 5:4)*

Song: This is God's world

Opening the Word

The Leader should indicate which of the following forms will be taken to reflect on the biblical texts.

a) *People turn to each other and share which of the above texts they most or least appreciate and why.*

b) *People sit in silence for five minutes as music is played, after which anyone may briefly share what has occurred to them as they reflected on the texts.*

c) *One person may offer a short homily on any of the texts.*

A song may be sung.

Response

Leader: What, at this moment, does God require of us?

Do we need to offer our gratitude for the nourishment for body, soul and mind which the earth provides?

Do we need to admit our failure to care for the earth as we should?

Do we need to make a positive commitment to renewing the health of the earth's environment?

In the next few minutes let us respond by silently reflecting on what is asked of us personally.

(Continue with the words below if the symbolic action is being included, gesturing to where each table is, on saying the words 'gratitude, regret, commitment'.)

While some music plays, you may, if you wish, go to whichever table most represents what you feel called to do, whether that be to express gratitude, regret or commitment.

At your chosen table, you may choose to light a votive light from the large candle and place it prayerfully on the table, as a sign of your response to God.

Prayer *(from the United Nations Sabbath Programme)*

Leader: Eternal God,
give us hearts to understand
never to take from creation's beauty
more than we can give,
never to destroy wantonly
for the furtherance of greed,
never to deny to give our hands
for the building of earth's beauty,
never to take from her what we cannot use.

ALL: **Give us hearts to understand**
that to destroy earth's music
is to create confusion,
that to wreck her appearance
is to blind us to beauty,
that to callously pollute her fragrance
is to make a house of stench,
and that as we care for her,
she will care for us.
Amen.

For the COP26 Conference:

Leader: Loving Creator,
at this moment in earth's history
when humanity must take account of earth's destiny,
give to those leaders who gather in Glasgow
a sense of urgency,
a perception of necessity
and the wisdom and will
to secure the health and well-being of the world
at whatever the cost to wealth,
political advantage or prestige.

ALL: **And give to us all a vision**
of a world restored to full health
that is worthy of all those yet to be born
and worth all the work, sacrifice and commitment

which is ours to offer.
Amen.

Affirmation *(standing)*

Leader: We believe that this is God's world
and all that lives on it;
ALL: **we believe that living gratefully**
and giving generously are marks of faith.

Leader: We believe that all of humanity
should have equal access to the earth's resources,
ALL: **and that every individual must now act**
to preserve this world
so that the children of tomorrow
will not be burdened by the mistakes of today.

Leader: And so we commit ourselves
ALL: **to think globally,**
to trade fairly,
to live responsibly,
and to love this world as it is loved by God,
who in Christ became one with creation.
Amen.

Closing song

Dismissal

Leader: Now go in peace
to enjoy the earth,
and care for creation
in partnership with God,
who in Christ
has honoured and blessed us.
Amen.

The Wild Goose Resource Group, in consultation with the Iona Community's Common Concern Network on the Environment

Appendix

This is God's world

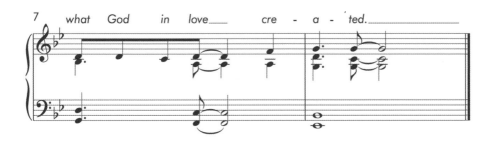

On the eighth day

Leader C (as per liturgy) introduces this with the words below. Thereafter two voices – the narrator and God – read the script. They should not stand close to each other, and if either acoustics or amplification allows, the voice of God could come from the back of the gathering.

Leader: We are now going to hear a reading entitled *On the eighth day*.

It is an imaginary sequel to the story
at the beginning of Genesis in which
God creates the world in seven stages.
Before and after each section of the reading
we will sing Kyrie Eleison (Lord, have mercy)
but we begin by reminding ourselves of the delight
God felt when the work of creation was done.

God saw all that had been made,
and it was very good.
Evening and morning came,
the sixth day.

Thus the heavens and the earth
and everything in them was completed.
On the sixth day
God made an end to the work,
and on the seventh day, having finished,
God blessed the day and made it holy,
because it was the day which marked
the completion of the work of creation.

Narrator: After the making of heaven and earth,
and after the time of resting,
and after the Word had returned from being flesh,
and after the Spirit's sending,
God gazed in love on creation.

And behold,
the world had lost its innocence
and thick darkness brooded everywhere.

Kyrie Eleison

On the eighth day,
God looked on humanity
and humanity was in a mess –

emaciated by hunger,
bloated by excess,
maimed by war,
blinded by bigotry.

The guardians of the earth seemed to serve
their basest desires and stumbled towards the abyss.

And God said,

God: What has happened to the children I lifted to my cheek,
whose names are written on the palms of my hands?

This is not good.
I call on the evening and I call on the morning
to witness my displeasure;
and I long for a different day.

Kyrie Eleison

Narrator: On the ninth day,
God looked on earth's creatures,
and earth's creatures were in a mess –

fish riddled with cancers,
birds deprived of their habitat,
the beasts of the wild hunted as trophies,
the beasts of the field penned up in factories.

And God said,

God: Where now is the swallow who nested in my house?
Where now is the donkey which carried my son?

This is not good.
I call on the evening and I call on the morning
to witness my displeasure;
and I long for a different day.

> *Kyrie Eleison*

Narrator: On the tenth day,
God looked at the sky,
and the sky was in a mess –

> the ozone layer was no longer friendly,
> weather systems had lost their predictability,
> the stars which symbolised the harmony of heaven
> feared for the militarisation of the galaxy.

And God said,

God: Has the sunset lost its fascination?
Must the tapestry be torn which I carefully embroidered?

This is not good.
I call on the evening and I call on the morning
to witness my displeasure;
and I long for a different day.

> *Kyrie Eleison*

Narrator: On the eleventh day,
God looked at the produce of the soil,
and the produce of the soil was in a mess –

> fields meant to feed the hungry
> were planted with cash crops
> for 'civilised' cravings,
> pastures had become deserts
> through constant over-grazing,
> rainforests disappeared
> through a lust for easy money.

And God said,

God: Where are the lilies better dressed than Solomon?
        Where is the buzzing of bees?

        This is not good.
        I call on the evening and I call on the morning
        to witness my displeasure;
        and I long for a different day.

            Kyrie Eleison

Narrator: On the twelfth day,
           God looked at the land and the sea;
           and the land and sea were in a mess –

               contaminated by waste,
               debilitated by detergent,
               fouled by artificial fertiliser,
               drained of natural goodness.

        And God said,

God: How can the valleys laugh and sing?
        How can the deep seas roar?
        How can the mountains skip like rams
        if nature is in mourning?

        This is not good.
        I call on the evening and I call on the morning
        to witness my displeasure;
        and I long for a different day.

            Kyrie Eleison

Narrator: On the thirteenth day,
           God looked at light and darkness;
           and light and darkness were in a mess –

               truth was in exile,

honesty was belittled,
cheap pleasure wore the mantle meant for love,
and the religion of the privileged
was proclaimed heir to the throne
of the saviour of the poor.

And God said,

God: Who can believe what I have seen?
To whom did I think I had revealed my power?

This is not good.
I call on the evening and I call on the morning
to witness my displeasure;
and I long for a different day.

Kyrie Eleison

Narrator: On the fourteenth day,
God looked away from the world
which had been created out of love
and shaped with deep beauty,

and God wept.

Kyrie Eleison

Narrator: When the time of weeping was done,
God said,

God: I have kept faith with the children of earth,
but they do not keep faith with me.

I have promised and given
nature's kindly gifts,
asking that they be treated well,
enjoyed and shared.
I have promised and given
deep fulfilment in life,
· asking for the safeguarding of creation

that her abundance may keep flowing.

O, children of earth,
you who have witnessed my love,
how little I witness of yours!

In silence I wait;
I plead and I wait.
Do not grieve me.
Let there be light from this darkness!
Let me witness your love!

I long for that different day.

Wild Goose Resource Group

Sources and acknowledgements

'God's Good Earth: A Service of Worship in Preparation for the COP26 Climate Change Conference', and 'On the eighth day' © Wild Goose Resource Group, Iona Community, Suite 9 Fairfield, 1048 Govan Road, Glasgow, G51 4XS, Scotland T: 0141 429 7281; www.wildgoose.scot

'This is God's world' © Wild Goose Resource Group, Iona Community, Suite 9 Fairfield, 1048 Govan Road, Glasgow, G51 4XS, Scotland T: 0141 429 7281; www.wildgoose.scot

The Wild Goose Resource Group (WGRG) exists to enable and equip congregations and clergy in the shaping and creation of new forms of worship that are relevant, contextual and participatory.

The group is a project of the Iona Community, consisting of John L. Bell and Jo Love (Resource Workers) and Gail Ullrich (Administrator). We were founded over 30 years ago by John L. Bell and the late Graham Maule.

We work in the UK and throughout the world leading workshops, conferences and worship. We also create and publish songs, liturgies and recordings, often in collaboration with the Wild Goose Collective, an ad hoc gathering of our musical friends.

Our work brings curiosity and creativity, exploration and perception, to liturgy and worship, music and song, prayer and politics, engagement and devotion.

For more information: www.wildgoose.scot

Liturgical resources

Calls to worship /opening responses and prayers

Gathering responses

Mother and Father of all life, God-with-us, we gather:
to begin again our stewardship of your creation.

Feed us:
with knowledge and understanding.

Awaken within our hearts:
a passion for sustainable living.

Enable us:
to take lighter footsteps on your good earth.

Help us:
to find ways of living more simply.

Stuart Elliott

Call to worship

Praise God, all you people of the earth.
Blessed be God forever.
From the rising of the sun to its setting
blessed be God forever.
As high as the tree soaring above the forest,
as beautiful as the river flowing through many lands,
as rich as the ecosystems of an abundant earth,
as close as the smallest creature on the ground,
so good is the God of all creation.
blessed be God forever.

Kathy Galloway

Strengthen us, Mother God

Mothering God,
we come to worship
within your renewing love.
So strengthen and encourage us,
that we see the next steps for action,
and have the courage to take them.
For your love's sake.
Amen.

Chris Polhill

Prayers of approach

A Celtic rune of hospitality

We saw a stranger yesterday.
We put food in the eating place,
drink in the drinking place,
music in the listening place.

And in the sacred name of the triune God,
she blessed us and our house,
our cattle and our dear ones.
As the lark says in her song:
Often, often, often
goes the Christ in the stranger's guise.

God of all life

God of all life,
beyond our imagining, and yet coming so close;
you refuse to leave those in need on the rubbish dump.
You give the poor a place of dignity among the powerful.
You make a home for the homeless,
and bring joy abounding to families and communities.

As we gather to celebrate and give thanks for your harvest of blessing,
may we live within your reality,
share your vision,
and do your will,
that the whole earth may echo your glory.

Have mercy on us, God.
Grant us the wisdom
to be still enough to notice
that the cycles of life
intertwining us all
have a fragile strength
and we are all diminished in their breaking.
We pray in the name of Jesus.
AMEN.

Kathy Galloway

Confession/repentance/absolution

Free us for action

Each verse and response could be said at a different point in a service.

Loving God, in Jesus you stepped up to the line,
bit the bullet, owned the problem.
Walk beside us as we seek to accept the evidence
that the earth is under threat.
Share our pain for the way we have avoided the truth
and ignored the signs,
and free us from the guilt that binds us.

Loving God, in Jesus you laid yourself open, stuck your neck out,
and made yourself vulnerable to the whims of earthly rulers.
Walk beside us as we risk the consequences of self-examination.
Share our pain for what has been done in self-seeking and blindness,
and free us from the guilt that binds us.

Loving God, in Jesus you faced the music,
carried the can, took the blame.
Walk beside us as we seek to accept our part in damaging the earth.
Share our pain for what has been done in foolishness and ignorance,
and free us from the guilt that binds us.

Loving God, in Jesus you grasped the nettle, picked up the shovel,
became involved.
Walk beside us as we struggle to change our lives.
Share our pain for what has not been done through fear and weakness,
and free us from the guilt that binds us.

John Polhill

John Polhill is a member of the Iona Community who works voluntarily in the Environmental Team of Lichfield Church of England Diocese. In 1999, John and his wife, Christine, bought a home on the edge of Cannock Chase (20 miles north of Birmingham). In the grounds of this property they have created a series of themed gardens on the Christian spiritual journey and environmental issues. The gardens and meeting space/retreat accommodation are used regularly by individuals and groups (www.reflectiongardens.org.uk).

We did not know

We are grateful, Creator God,
for all the benefits extracted from land and sea,
for all the people who have risked their lives for our comfort,
our health, our wealth, our mobility.

We did not know, God who is with us in our darkness,
we did not know the cost to our radiant planet.
We did not wish to know, God who illumines our darkness,
we did not wish to know the cost to your people;
health destroyed, communities ruined, land degraded,
children labouring, conflicts raging.

For the sin we could not confess,
for the sin we did not confess,
for the sin we chose not to confess;

Lord have mercy upon us.
Christ have mercy upon us.
Lord have mercy upon us.

Kathy Galloway

Meditations

If we had but a glimpse

If we had but a glimpse of the world as a resting place, would we be caught in the sacred story? Honoured as the whole of life becomes a day of preparation. We might just then become co-creators of the dawn for a divine re-imagining of the lost art and beauty of creation. A life laid fallow, for a time, is not in vain. To let go, to allow the natural restfulness to rise up and with gentle ease, to participate, earthed once again.

Stuart Elliott

Wow!

Wow, God!
You did good making this planet!
It's beautiful, amazing –
from tiny wriggly things,
to trees and mountains,
and people of all races,
extraordinary people,

Just sorry!
For the mess we make.
The whole me first,
humans are tops thing;
the rows, and the violence,
no feeling for being part
of something so much bigger.

Help! Please!
We can't see how to do it,
how to undo the mess we've made,
how to work together.
How to love your way,
earth and sea and human,
and how we fit together.

We could?
Find a gentle way,
give stuff up, take things on;
live a way of healing?
Reminds me now of Jesus,
his inclusive way of love.

Chris Polhill

The Wow of creation

Each of us made of stardust –
atoms built millions of years ago in hot stars,
thrown randomly into space,
collected by all-pervading gravity
and taken in as food, drink, air,
and recycled again by nature;
spread out for reuse,
during our lifetimes and after.

Start with a hydrogen atom
and an oxygen atom or two,
and carbon atoms for fire and fuel;
add nitrogen atoms and the stage is set
for the finger of God to bring the chemistry to life –
DNA molecules which can reproduce,
but only when living in community with others.

When you think of the simplicity of the basic building blocks of the universe,
such as the hydrogen atom –
and the fact that its potential for change is limited
to the rise and fall of its energy levels,
and reflect that with this are made:

the hummingbird and the whale
the mind of an Einstein
the words of Mandela
the landscape of South Africa
the laughter of children
the courage of people in suffering,
then no miracle
no sign
can ever arouse more wonder
than the facts of the natural universe
and the mystery of the human soul.
Dust to dust
Atoms to atoms
We all share the atoms again and again.
When you eat and drink you become one with those atoms –
you receive what you already are,
you become more of what you already are.
Some of the atoms in your body may once have been part of a dinosaur.

When you breathe in, you breathe life-giving oxygen atoms –
do you breathe in some of the atoms that Jesus breathed?

David Hawkey

During his work life, David Hawkey was a science technology teacher who loved sharing the deep magic of creation with children – and was always learning from them. David is an associate member of the Iona Community living in England.

A lamentation and prayer of contrition to the whole of creation

1   [*To the heavenly hosts and the Holy Ghost*] We have painted over the canvas of your starry skies

2   With neon and floodlights blinding us to our place in your creation.

3   Without sight, we can no longer hear your morning stars singing together.

4   Our hearts have grown cold and closed to the pulsars of eternal love.

5   We have inflicted violence on your creation, grievous wounds on your body.

6   We have monetised the commons and disavowed our kinship with all living things.

7   We enslaved non-human beings and severed their ties to the land.

8   We have denied water to the thirsty, bread to the hungry, shelter to the refugee.

9   We abandoned belief and made graven images to worship Mammon.

10 We no longer marvel at your bow in the sky and have broken humanity into petty pieces.

11 The colours in your rainbow would remind us how much you love diversity

12 And how each dewdrop glistens with potential in the unfolding dance of life.

For our sins against the biomes, genomes and creature homes, forgive us our trespasses, have mercy upon our souls.

13 [*To the cryosphere*] With your breath the ice is formed and watery expanses are frozen. *(Job 47:10)*

14 We have melted your cryosphere so that the great winds across the lands and ocean currents falter

15 Bringing drought and famine and cruel blasts of heat and cold against the creatures.

For our sins against the biomes, genomes and creature homes, forgive us our trespasses, have mercy upon our souls.

16 [*To the forests*] Woodlands once flourished like the forests of Lebanon *(Ps 72:16)* and the trees sang for joy. *(Ps 96:12)*

17 But now the towering trees of the forest cathedrals are felled to make toilet paper, with few left to rebuild your Temples.

18 The land is now desolate, stumps burning, the soil washing away with the monsoon, a wasteland bereft of creatures.

For our sins against the biomes, genomes and creature homes, forgive us our trespasses, have mercy upon our souls.

19 [*To the grasslands*] Where the wilderness grasslands overflowed, the hills were clothed with gladness. *(Ps 65:12)*

20 But now we weep and mourn for the grasslands on the mountain; we sing a mournful song for the pastures in the wilderness.

21 Because they are so scorched no one travels through them; the sound of livestock is no longer heard there.

22 Even the birds in the sky and the wild animals in the fields have fled and are gone. *(Jer 9:10)*

For our sins against the biomes, genomes and creature homes, forgive us our trespasses, have mercy upon our souls.

23 [*To the deserts*] You brought us into a good land, with brooks of water, fountains that spring out of valleys and hills. *(Deut 8:7)*

24 Where the desert and the dry land rejoiced, celebrated and blossomed like crocuses. *(Isa 35:1)*

25 And we have become like a shrub in the desert, trying to grow in a salt land where nothing can live. *(Jer 17:6)*

For our sins against the biomes, genomes and creature homes, forgive us our trespasses, have mercy upon our souls.

26 [*To the freshwater and wetlands*] You caused springs to gush forth into rivers that flow between the mountains. *(Ps 104:10)*

27 And the rivers clapped their hands and the mountains shouted together for joy. *(Ps 98:8)*

28 We lived like a tree planted by the rivers of water that brought forth fruit in its season, and its leaves did not wither. *(Ps 1:3)*

29 Until the rivers were aflame with our petrochemicals and our fertilisers poisoned your water creatures.

For our sins against the biomes, genomes and creature homes, forgive us our trespasses, have mercy upon our souls.

30 [*To the oceans*] You made the sea great and broad, with swarms of life without number, creatures both small and great. *(Ps 104:25)*

31 We have plundered your bounty, and polluted your seas with plastic and chemicals.

32 The oceans' great creatures groan and beach themselves from the noise pollution of our invasive vessels.

For our sins against the biomes, genomes and creature homes, forgive us our trespasses, have mercy upon our souls.

33 [*To the firstborn peoples*] We ask forgiveness of our brothers and sisters, the Native Peoples

34 For bringing disease and death upon their totem clans, communities and cities.

35 We have plundered their sacred groves and disturbed their ancestors in their rest

36 And denigrated and desecrated their ancient knowledge and wisdom.

37 We confess that it has taken centuries for our binary science

38 To confirm that their beliefs and values were in harmony with the whole creation.

39 And that, as they warned us, we have become possessed by our possessions.

40 Intoxicated with hubris, greed and selfishness.

41 Convinced of our separateness and superiority.

For our sins against the biomes, genomes and creature homes, forgive us our trespasses, have mercy upon our souls.

42 We repent and seek redemption.

43 With humility we pray for healing and commit our labours to peace.

44 May our faith going forward be as a grain of mustard seed, planted in your garden,

45 Growing into a Tree of Life, that the birds of the air will make their homes once again in its branches. *(Luke 13:19)*

46 May we be keepers of the commons, in the Nowness of your vast and beautiful creation

47 That we might come to be in right relations with all creatures walking the twofold way that carries us home to you, the Creator *(Wis 13:5)*

48 And perfuses your stillness throughout our hearts forever.

49 In your name, our loving landlord, we pray and we act in community.

50 You above all and others above ourselves.

51 We could say more but could never say enough; let the final word be: Saleh. *(Sir 43:27)*

For our sins against the biomes, genomes and creature homes, forgive us our trespasses, have mercy upon our souls.
Saleh.

Richard A. Nisbett

The 51 lines of the prayer commemorate 51 Earth Days since the original Earth Day in 1970.

Prayers/litanies of thanksgiving

Generous God

Generous God,
You are the source of all that is, creating and sustaining every living thing.
You are the source of all food, material and spiritual,
nourishing us in both body and soul.
You are the river of life for our thirst.
You love the world so much that you sent your only Son.
May we be filled with your breath,
nourished by your food,
renewed by your living water
and sustained by your love.

Creator God, we give thanks
that we have heard the Spirit of God in the freshening leaves
and the rush of water.
So we pray for the creation which nourishes and sustains all that lives.
Renew in us the sense of its value
that we may not squander its riches,
or so bend it to our will that we find we have destroyed it.

We pray for all whose experience of water is not of blessing but of curse;
as the monsoon rains fall relentlessly from the skies,
as rivers burst their banks, bridges are swept away and dams crumble,
as ice-caps melt and flash floods sweep down
carrying destruction over innumerable miles,
there is water everywhere, and none of it is clean.
We see thirst that can find only filthy water to drink,
waterborne and skin diseases,
the drowning of people and animals.

Christ, draw near to them,
ordinary people, trembling and most wretched,
rowing through the infinite storm of this age;

and bring them safely
to the most beautiful haven of life.
All-compassionate God,
deliver your people.

Kathy Galloway

Thank you for ordinary wonderful things

Thank you, God, for the colour of tomatoes and beetroot,
for the different colours and shapes and fragrances of flowers,
for grubby potatoes and funny-shaped carrots –
for the goodness of the earth itself.

Thank you, God, for the taste of apples from the tree –
of blackberries picked straight from the hedgerow;
for the glossiness of conkers and acorns …

Thank you, God, for the smell of baking cakes and real coffee.
For the smell of woodsmoke and damp leaves;
and for the lights of home on a dark evening.

Thank you, God, for the kiss of a dog's wet nose and
for the purring contentedness of a cat.

For all of these ordinary wonderful things – thank you, God.
May we never forget to give thanks to you, Maker and Giver of all.
Amen.

Richard Sharples

Richard Sharples is a Methodist minister in Bristol, who seeks ways of weaving gardening into his ministry. He is a member of the Iona Community.

Prayer

Tonight, let us be grateful for changing things:
for cloud patterns and seasonal landscapes,
for the restless sea and multi-coloured earth,
for branch and leaf and fruit and flower,
for rocks, weather-carved like an old face which could tell stories,
for wind and water and all that was never meant to stand still,
for the lilies waving in the field.
This is your economy, Lord.
Teach us its value.

Set up your cross in the marketplaces of our world,
to remind us of your love for the unproductive, the imperfect and the lost,
and of the malice of human greed.
Redeem our souls,
redeem our peoples,
redeem our times.

We pray in the name of Jesus Christ,
through whose passion and death
the treasure house of the kingdom was opened to all.
Amen.

John L. Bell

Rainbow litany

When the rainbow appears in the clouds, I will see it and remember the ever-lasting covenant between me and all living beings on earth. That is the sign of the promise which I am making to all living beings. (Genesis 9:16–17)

Let us remember the sign of your promise,
the diversity built into the very fabric of your creation,
the colours of our lives, of our creativity, of our hope in you.

Green is the colour of the earth after rain.
Let it be for us a sign of growth and new life

Yellow is the colour of the harvest corn.
Let it be for us a sign of sufficiency and sharing.

Red is the colour of wild berries.
Let it be for us a sign of suffering and courage.

Orange is the colour of pumpkin and spices and squash.
Let it be for us a sign of gift and rejoicing.

Blue is the colour of the sky above us and the sea around us.
Let it be for us a symbol of power and peace.

Violet is the colour of the small flowers clinging to mountain rock.
Let it be for us a sign of kindness and care.

Purple is the colour of the night just before dawn.
Let it be for us a sign of our longing and our hope in Christ.

(An Alleluia or Gloria may be said or sung between each colour. Banners or flags of appropriate colours may also be raised or presented.)

Kathy Galloway

Prayers of intercession and concern

God of all creation

God of all creation,
and of all creatures,
we pray today for the peacemakers, for the seekers of justice,
for people of goodwill who risk much, sometimes their lives,
to stand in solidarity across many dividing lines and barriers.
We pray for those who have lost loved ones to violence,
and for safety, security, human rights and dignity for all,
not just for some.
We pray for the courage to continue working together
for a world of justice, peace and equality.
Loving God,
hear our prayer.

God of all creation,
we give you thanks for agreements that safeguard the environment.
We pray for those who seek to make this a reality,
especially those following up on climate change agreements
made in Paris in 2015.
May their efforts be fruitful.
Loving God,
hear our prayer.

God of all creation,
we remember those who are far from power.
We pray for
those vulnerable in the face of flood and drought, wind and weather,
those vulnerable in the face of impersonal global markets,
those crying out for help and justice in times of distress.
Loving God,
hear our prayer.

May all of us be inspired by the Word that makes all things new;
to speak words of truth,
words of dignity,

words of peace,
words of life,
in the name of the Word who became flesh.
Amen.

Kathy Galloway

Together we stand strong

Creator God,
Life of life,
we give thanks for persistent people everywhere:
small farmers feeding most of the world,
people setting up seed banks, maintaining biodiversity,
and never giving up in the struggle for climate justice.
We are connected with seven billion people,
in a global community of trade, food, habitat.
Give us courage and faith to put ourselves on the line for climate justice
for we are each of us one in a million.
Together we stand strong.

Brother Christ
who came to share our lives, to encourage and liberate us.
You live amongst us all.
We give thanks for dedicated people everywhere,
challenging abuses of power, exposing corrupt practices
and never giving up in the struggle for climate justice.
May we play our part in challenging greed and wastefulness,
creating more sustainable communities,
and treading more lightly on the earth.
For we are each of us one in a million.
Together we stand strong.

Spirit of God,
who works among people,
who moves our hearts and lives with love.
We give thanks for the people and places we care about.
And we pray for all who suffer anguish for the people and places they love,

for all whose livelihoods are threatened by a changing climate,
for all who work to improve the future for all our children.
May we join our voices in tears of protest and songs of hope,
and never give up in the struggle for climate justice.
For we are each of us one in a million.
Together we stand strong.

O Holy Trinity,
whose promise is of a life
where all will flourish and be respected,
we pray that, as we live by your grace and sharing,
we may be led to use less energy,
buy more locally,
share resources more wisely
and enable our politicians to speak out for climate justice.
For we are each of us one in a million.
Together we stand strong.

Kathy Galloway

Communion of saints

A prayer from Iona Abbey

Creator God,
we give thanks for people and organisations
working to care for the earth:
God bless all those who know the true value of the land
and have the courage and faith to put themselves on the line.

God bless the Greenbelt Movement in Kenya, and Wangari Maathai,
winner of the Nobel Peace Prize in 2004.
God bless the women of the Chipko movement in India,
who halt commercial logging by hugging trees.

(Invite participants to name other past and present saints who have witnessed to the integrity of creation.)

God bless …

Neil Paynter, from a liturgy in Iona Abbey

Neil Paynter was a member of the Resident Group on Iona and is an associate of the Iona Community.

Prayers of self-offering/commitment

A new heaven and a new earth

Creating God, you have given us a vision of a new heaven and a new earth:
resources conserved
earth tended
atmosphere cleansed
trees planted
injustice ended
oceans teeming
nations at peace.
Creator, Redeemer, Sustainer,
alert nations, enthuse churches,
receive our commitment and so entwine our lives with your purpose that
earth and heaven sing of your glory.

John Harrison

John Harrison was a member of the Iona Community and frequent volunteer on Iona who, with his wife, Marion, tried to practise what he preached – organic gardening, solar water heating, solar photovoltaic electrical generation and the 4 Rs – reduce, reuse, repair, recycle. John died in 2020.

Prayers to go/blessing/benedictions

A Gaelic blessing

Deep peace of the running wave to you
Deep peace of the flowing air to you
Deep peace of the quiet earth to you
Deep peace of the shining stars to you
Deep peace of the Son of peace to you

Blessing

Let us go out giving thanks for the good earth.
Blessed be God forever.
Let us go out in unity with all who seek to preserve the earth.
Blessed be God forever.
Let us go out in the conviction that change is possible
and climate disaster is not inevitable.
Blessed be God forever.
And the blessing of God the Creator, Christ the Redeemer and the Spirit,
the Sustainer of all life,
be with us, and with all the peoples of the earth, now and always.
Amen.

Kathy Galloway

Blessing

Go in peace,
and be witnesses to hope.
May God bless us with strength to seek justice.
May God bless us with wisdom to care for the earth.
May God bless us with love to bring forth new life.
Amen.

Blessing

Bless to us, O God,
the moon that is above us,
the earth that is beneath us,
the friends who are around us,
your image deep within us.
Evermore of evermore,
bless to us our rest.

From the *Carmina Gadelica*

Additional resources

Additional resources can be found in A Heart for Creation: Worship Resources and Reflections on the Environment, *by Chris Polhill, Wild Goose Publications.*

Additional special full liturgies:

Celebrating Love for All God's Creation: An All-age Communion Service for the Feast of Saint Francis (including a blessing of animals), by Nancy Cocks, Wild Goose Publications

Iona Abbey Creation Liturgy 1, Iona Community, Wild Goose Publications

Iona Abbey Creation Liturgy 2, Iona Community, Wild Goose Publications

We Will Tread the Earth Lightly: A Service of Lamentation to Liberate Us for Action, by Chris Polhill, Wild Goose Publications

See www.ionabooks.com

Sources and acknowledgements

'The Wow of creation', by David Hawkey, from *Holy Ground: Liturgies and Worship Resources for an Engaged Spirituality*, Neil Paynter and Helen Boothroyd (Eds), Wild Goose Publications, 2005

'Thank you for ordinary wonderful things', by Richard Sharples, from *A Heart for Creation: Worship Resources and Reflections on the Environment*, Chris Polhill, Wild Goose Publications, 2010

'Prayer', by John L. Bell, © Wild Goose Resource Group, Iona Community, Suite 9 Fairfield, 1048 Govan Road, Glasgow, G51 4XS, Scotland T: 0141 429 7281; www.wildgoose.scot

'A prayer from Iona Abbey', by Neil Paynter, from 'Crucified earth: A service of prayers for the environment', Iona Abbey, 2000, by Neil Paynter, from *Holy Ground: Liturgies and Worship Resources for an Engaged Spirituality*, Neil Paynter and Helen Boothroyd (Eds), Wild Goose Publications, 2005

'A new heaven and a new earth', from 'Footprints in the Cosmos', by John Harrison, from *Holy Ground: Liturgies and Worship Resources for an Engaged Spirituality*, Neil Paynter and Helen Boothroyd (Eds), Wild Goose Publications, 2005

Hymns and songs

Introduction

For each of the twelve weeks of the Christian Year covered by this book, that is, the five weeks of Creation Time and the remaining weeks of the Christian Year (B), the editors have selected one song by John L. Bell and the Wild Goose Resource Group, and by two other Community members. These songs relate to the lectionary readings and reflections for each week. They can either be sung to well-known tunes, or the tunes are easily available.

The Wild Goose Resource Group of the Iona Community has produced numerous song collections which include suitable songs for Creation Time and for worship with an environmental focus. These can be found on the Wild Goose Publications website: www.ionabooks.com

There are many good hymns, songs and chants suitable for worship with a focus on the earth our home, and on care for and the integrity of creation. Apart from denominational hymn and songbooks, the best way to discover more and new songs is through hymnary.org. This is *'a comprehensive index of over 1 million hymn texts, hymn tunes and hymnals, with information and indices on authors and composers, lyrics and scores of many hymns, and various media files'*.

Kathy Galloway

1. God, in creating, bore and blessed

Words: John L. Bell, copyright © 2002 WGRG, Iona Community.
Tune: MARY MORRISON or with 4-line verses GONFALON ROYAL,
or YE BANKS & BRAES

1. God, in creating, bore and blessed
   the sea to move, the land to rest,
   the wind to stir and silence both,
   the sun to shine and summon growth.
   God filled the world with living things
   conveyed by feet or fins or wings
   and then God charged humanity
   with care of air and land and sea.

2. Not as earth's lords but as its friends
   we're called to care as God intends:
   the fertile fields to till and groom,
   the desert wastes to bring to bloom;
   and through technology and skill
   the hungry of the world to fill
   with what God made their right to be –
   the nourishment of earth and sea.

3. Yet avarice has made us blind
   to suffering earth and humankind,
   as science, soured in thought and deed,
   serves profit, pride or human greed.
   Fauna and flora wilt and die,
   pollution threatens soil and sky,
   and selfish nations disagree
   on how to treat air, land and sea.

4. O God, who wills that we be wise,
   confront our minds, our hearts, our eyes
   with how we desecrate our worth
   by fouling sea and raping earth.
   Shame and subdue our perverse skill
   in word to care, in fact to kill.

Redeem our stained technology
to mend and manage earth and sea.

5. Thus may the earth reclaim its good,
   supporting life, producing food,
   through healthy water, soil and air
   sustaining creatures everywhere.
   Then trees indeed shall clap their hands,
   and children safely sculpt the sands,
   and all shall honour heaven's decree
   and serve, as friends, air, land and sea.

2. The life of the world

Words: copyright © Kathy Galloway.
Tune: LIFE OF THE WORLD, Ian Galloway

1. Oh, the life of the world is a joy and a treasure,
   unfolding in beauty the green growing tree,
   the changing of seasons in mountain and valley,
   the stars and the bright restless sea.

2. Oh, the life of the world is a fountain of goodness,
   overflowing in labour and passion and pain,
   in the sound of the city and the silence of wisdom,
   in the birth of a child once again.

3. Oh, the life of the world is the source of our healing;
   it rises in laughter and wells up in song;
   it springs from the care of the poor and the broken
   and refreshes where justice is strong.

4. Oh, the life of the world is a promise of blessing,
   in the rain that renews in the heat of the sun;
   in the heart that confesses and the act that expresses
   all things and all people are one.

5. Oh, the life of the world is the breath of our being,
   it is fragile and precious and offers a choice;
   shall we share the earth wisely, can we touch the earth gently,
   will we listen to earth's silenced voice?

6. So give thanks for the life and give love to the Maker,
   and rejoice in the gift of the bright risen Son,
   and walk in the peace and the power of the Spirit,
   till the days of our living are done.

3. All the wonder that surrounds us

Words: John L. Bell & Graham Maule,
copyright © 2002, 2018 WGRG, Iona Community.
Tune: AR HYD Y NOS (All Through the Night)

1. All the wonder that surrounds us
   springs from God's care:
   all that marvels or confounds us,
   raw, rich or rare;
   touch and texture, sights and voices,
   nature's countless forms and choices,
   all for which the heart rejoices
   springs from God's care.

2. Every creature, every human
   lives by God's grace:
   every family, man and woman,
   culture and race;
   those whom fortune seems to favour,
   those exploited for their labour,
   those who need to know a neighbour
   live by God's grace.

3. How can we revere God's goodness
   meant for all time?
   How ensure that each uniqueness
   keeps in its prime?
   How can we revere with pleasure
   all God gives for life and leisure,
   how preserve each earthly treasure
   meant for all time?

4. God has willed that peace and justice
   walk hand in hand.
   These, with love, shall build foundations
   on which we'll stand:
   love for lover, friend and stranger,
   love defying death and danger,
   love as first born in a manger –
   heaven close at hand.

4. The sorrow

1. Don't tell me of a faith that fears
   to face the world around;
   don't dull my mind with fickle thoughts
   of grace without a ground.

Chorus: I need to know that God is real,
I need to know that Christ can feel
the need to touch and love and heal
the world, including me.

2. Don't speak of piety and prayers
   divorced from human need;
   don't talk of spirit without flesh
   like harvest without seed.

3. Don't sate my soul with common sense
   distilled from ages past,
   inept for those who fear the world's
   about to breathe its last.

4. Don't set the cross before my eyes
   unless you tell the truth
   of how the Lord who finds the lost
   was often found uncouth.

5. So, let the Gospel come alive,
   in actions plain to see
   in imitation of the one
   whose love extends to me.

If using Kingsfold, omit the chorus, put together vs 1 & 2 and 3 & 4, and
for the last four lines after verse 5, add this adaptation of the chorus:

I need to know that God is real
and know that Christ can see
the need to touch and love and heal
the world, including me.

5. We will not take what is not ours

Words: John L. Bell & Graham Maule,
copyright © 1989, 1997 WGRG, Iona Community.
Tune: 8TH COMMANDMENT (from the collections Love from Below *and*
Love & Anger) *or WINCHESTER NEW or TALLIS' CANON*

1. We will not take what is not ours:
   the freedom of a separate place,
   the future of a different race,
   the unrestrictiveness of space.

2. We will not take what is not ours:
   the need to fulfil love's demand,
   the right to contradict the smooth,
   the claim of youth to understand.

3. We will not take what is not ours
   nor ravage, exploit or pollute
   till nature mourns her barren state,
   and justice limps both blind and mute.

4. We will not take what is not ours
   and offer then to heaven the dross
   of poverty caused by our greed
   to win despite our neighbour's loss.

5. We will not take what is not ours
   nor dare to enslave or disown
   that loyalty of heart and mind
   which is a gift for God alone.

If using 8TH COMMANDMENT, at the end of each verse repeat the line: We will
not take what is not ours.

6. I will sing a song of love

Words: John L. Bell, copyright © 2005 WGRG, Iona Community.
Tune: NAMED AND KNOWN (from the collection I Will Not Sing Alone)

Chorus: I will sing a song of love
to the one who first loved me,
and I'll sing it as a child of God
who is named and known and free.
For the love of God is good,
it is broad and deep and long,
and above all else that matters
God is worthy of my song.

1. And I will not sing alone
   but with earth and sky and sea,
   for creation raised its voice
   well in advance of me.

2. And I'll sing with every soul,
   every language, every race,
   which proclaims this world is good
   for God has blessed this place.

3. And I'll sing for what is right
   and against all that is wrong,
   because God is never neutral
   who inspires my song.

4. As I bring to God my joy,
   so I'll bring to God my pain
   for there is no hurt which God
   requires me to retain.

5. While my life on earth still runs,
   may my song to God be given,
   till through grace I join the harmony
   of all in heaven.

7. Monarch and maker of all time and space

Words: John L. Bell, copyright © 2018 WGRG, Iona Community.
Tune: WOODLANDS or HIGHLAND CATHEDRAL

1. Monarch and maker of all time and space,
   sculptor of mountain and of desert place,
   source and sustainer of both sea and land,
   all that exists was crafted by your hand.

2. Yours are the myriad stars and cosmic grace,
   yours is the image in each human face;
   history and mystery in all that we know,
   yours is the love through which we live and grow.

3. Help us as guardians of all life on earth
   both to respect the world and prize its worth;
   and, in deep gratitude for all you give,
   turn greed to sharing so that all may live.

4. Glory to God to whom all praise is due,
   glory to Jesus making all things new,
   glory to God the Spirit, bold and bright,
   who leads the world through darkness into light.

8. Inspired by love and anger

Words: John L. Bell & Graham Maule,
copyright © 1987, 1997, 2018 WGRG, Iona Community.
Tune: SALLEY GARDENS or ELLACOMBE (Hosanna Loud Hosanna)

* Verses 3 & 4 may be omitted

1. Inspired by love and anger,
    disturbed by need and pain,
    informed of God's own bias,
    we ask this once again:
    'How long must some folk suffer?
    How long can few folk mind?
    How long dare vain self-interest
    turn prayer and pity blind?'

2. From those forever victims
    of heartless human greed,
    their cruel plight composes a
    litany of need:
    'Where are the fruits of justice?
    Where are the signs of peace?
    When is the day when prisoners
    and dreams find their release?'

*3. From those forever shackled
    to what their wealth can buy,
    the fear of lost advantage
    provokes the bitter cry,
    'Don't query our position!
    Don't criticise our wealth!
    Don't mention those exploited
    by politics and stealth!'

*4. To God, who through the prophets
    proclaimed a different age,
    we offer earth's indifference,
    its agony and rage:

'When will the wrongs be righted?
When will the kingdom come?
When will the world be generous
to all instead of some?'

5. God asks, 'Who will go for me?
Who will extend my reach?
And who, when few will listen,
will prophesy and preach?
And who, when few will welcome,
will offer all they know?
And who, when few will follow,
will walk the road I show?'

6. Amused in someone's kitchen,
asleep in someone's boat,
attuned to what the ancients
exposed, proclaimed and wrote,
a saviour without safety,
a tradesman without tools
has come to tip the balance
with fishermen and fools.

9. Sing praise to God on mountain tops

Words: John L. Bell & Graham Maule,
copyright © 1989, 2018 WGRG, Iona Community.
Tune: THE VICAR OF BRAY or HOW CAN I KEEP FROM SINGING?

1. Sing praise to God on mountain tops
    and in earth's lowest places,
    from blue lagoon to polar waste,
    from ocean to oasis.
    No random rock produced this world
    but God's own will and wonder.
    Thus hills rejoice and valleys sing
    and clouds concur with thunder.

2. Sing praise to God where grasses grow
    and flowers display their beauty,
    where Nature weaves her myriad web
    through love as much as duty.
    The seasons in their cycle speak
    of earth's complete provision.
    Let nothing mock inherent good
    or treat it with derision.

3. Sing praise to God where fishes swim
    and birds fly in formation,
    where animals of every kind
    diversify creation.
    All life that finds its home on earth
    is meant to be respected.
    Let nothing threaten, for base ends,
    what God through grace perfected.

4. Sing praise to God where humankind
    its majesty embraces,
    where different races, creeds and tongues
    distinguish different faces.
    God's image in each child of earth
    shall never pale or perish.
    So treat with love each human soul
    and thus God's goodness cherish.

10. Ageless God of boundless wonder

Words: John L. Bell, copyright © 2002, 2018 WGRG, Iona Community.
Tune: HOLY MANNA

1. Ageless God of boundless wonder,
   endless source of peerless grace
   who, to shatter speculation,
   came incarnate face to face;
   you we praise, almighty Maker,
   parent of humanity,
   power behind the powers we cherish,
   Lord of life as life should be.

2. None among us stood attentive
   when you brought the world to birth;
   nor can any claim full knowledge
   of the future states of earth.
   Fascinated, still we struggle
   to make sense of what has been,
   and with differing dreams imagine
   what, as yet, remains unseen.

3. Each idea still gestating,
   each conviction in its youth,
   each encounter, each engagement,
   each impassioned search for truth –
   these we offer, not for blessing
   but for shaping to your will.
   Here, good Lord, inspire, amaze us,
   fire our insight, fuse our skill.

4. Train our science to be servant
   of the needs we must perceive;
   teach our intellects, where blinded,
   that to see we must believe;
   in our politics prevent us
   from confusing means and ends;
   and through faith and doubt direct us
   to pursue what Christ intends.

11. The truth that sets us free

Words: John L. Bell, copyright © 2012, 2018 WGRG, Iona Community.
Tune: ESKE (from the collection The Truth That Sets Us Free*) or HYFRYDOL*

1. When the wheel of fate is turning
    and the mills of God grind slow,
    when the past seems more attractive
    than the future we don't know,
    when our confidence is waning
    and we lack security,
    comes the timeless word of Jesus
    that the truth will set us free.

2. Is it war or economics,
    is it danger or deceit,
    is it unforeseen depression,
    fear of failure to compete?
    Have the times which once were changing
    led where no one wants to be?
    Shall we live by lies on offer
    or the truth that sets us free?

3. With real faith there will be doubting,
    and with loss there will be grief.
    No one knows the contradictions
    which will exercise belief.
    Against conflicts life might bring us,
    God provides no guarantee,
    just this word of hope and healing:
    know that truth will set you free.

4. So, dear Jesus, make us willing
    to unmask convenient lies,
    to protest wherever power
    closes conscience, ears and eyes;
    and release our expectations
    of your kingdom yet to be,
    born in courage, joy and justice
    and the truth that sets us free.

12. Friends of Jesus, partnered with life

1. Friends of Christ Jesus: partnered with life;
   daughters and sons, and siblings who breathe
   the holy air, and bathe in seas
   of water from the depths of time.

2. God called our species into being:
   set forth our task of shepherding and care;
   though broken trust and selfish fraud
   have scarred the landscape of your love.

3. King now, we call you, Lord, and more;
   though from our dawn, you delegate:
   a servant Christ, Creation's friend,
   a wind that blows as sails unfurl.

4. Can we command the wind and waves?
   Can we make just injustice raw?
   Can we exploit and know no end?
   Alas, we've tried: a wounded world!

5. We need your help – this much is clear!
   And wisdom to use every gift.
   And listening to Creation's voice.
   And love, to bring fresh Good News home!

Sources of hymns and songs

1. GOD, IN CREATING, BORE AND BLESSED

Previously unpublished

2. THE LIFE OF THE WORLD

Church of Scotland Hymnary 4th Edition (Canterbury Press)
Ancient & Modern (Canterbury Press)
Singing the Faith (Canterbury Press)

3. ALL THE WONDER THAT SURROUNDS US

One Is The Body songbook/CD
Known Unknowns songbook

4. THE SORROW

Love & Anger songbook CD
Enemy of Apathy songbook

5. WE WILL NOT TAKE WHAT IS NOT OURS

Love & Anger songbook/CD
Love from Below songbook

6. I WILL SING A SONG OF LOVE

I Will Not Sing Alone songbook/CD

7. MONARCH AND MAKER OF ALL TIME AND SPACE

Known Unknowns songbook

8. INSPIRED BY LOVE AND ANGER

Love & Anger songbook/CD
Heaven Shall Not Wait songbook/CD
Known Unknowns songbook

9. SING PRAISE TO GOD ON MOUNTAIN TOPS

Love from Below songbook
Known Unknowns songbook

10. AGELESS GOD OF BOUNDLESS WONDER

One Is the Body songbook
Known Unknowns songbook

11. THE TRUTH THAT SETS US FREE

The Truth That Sets Us Free songbook/CD
Known Unknowns songbook

12. FRIENDS OF JESUS, PARTNERED WITH LIFE

Previously unpublished

The above Wild Goose collections are available from
www.wildgoose.scot or www.ionabooks.com

John L. Bell is a Resource Worker with the Iona Community, who lectures, preaches and conducts seminars across denominations. He is a hymn writer, author and occasional broadcaster, but retains a primary passion for congregational song. John is based in Glasgow and works with his colleagues in the Wild Goose Resource Group in the areas of music, worship and spirituality. The Group is an expression of the Iona Community's commitment to the renewal of public worship.

Resources

Links to faith-based community websites relating to the climate crisis

Global:

About the Season of Creation:
https://seasonofcreation.org

Act Alliance:
https://actalliance.org

Anglican Communion:
https://acen.anglicancommunion.org

Climate Justice/The Lutheran World Federation:
www.lutheranworld.org/climate-justice

World Communion of Reformed Churches:
http://wcrc.ch/justice/ecological

World Council of Churches:
www.oikoumene.org/what-we-do/care-for-creation-and-climate-justice

In Africa:

All Africa Conference of Churches:
www.aacc-ceta.org/en/programmes/peace-diakonia-and-development

Southern African Faith Communities' Environment Institute:
https://safcei.org

In Asia:

Christian Conference of Asia:
www.cca.org.hk/prophetic-diakonia-and-advocacy

In Australia:

Australia Religious Response to Climate Change:
www.arrcc.org.au

Climate Action Network Australia:
www.cana.net.au

In Canada:

Faith & the Common Good:
www.faithcommongood.org

Kairos: Faithful Action for Justice:
www.kairoscanada.org/what-we-do/ecological-justice

In Europe:

European Christian Environmental Network:
www.ecen.org/about-us

In the Netherlands:

De Huijberg:
https://dehuijberg.nl

Groenekerk:
https://www.groenekerken.nl

GroenGelovig:
https://groengelovig.nl

Inspiratietuinen:
https://inspiratie-tuinen.nl

Nederland A Rocha:
https://www.arocha.nl/nl

In the Pacific:

Pacific Conference of Churches:
www.pacificconferenceofchurches.org/about-us/our-key-programmes

In the UK:

Christian Aid Climate Campaign:
www.christianaid.org.uk/our-work/what-we-do/resilience-climate
www.christianaid.org.uk/pray/prayer-chain

Churches Together in Britain and Ireland:
https://ctbi.org.uk/environment-churches-and-christian-organisations

Eco Church: An A Rocha UK Project:
https://ecochurch.arocha.org.uk

Eco-Congregation Scotland:
www.ecocongregationscotland.org

Faith for the Climate:
https://faithfortheclimate.org.uk

In the USA:

Creation Justice Ministries
www.creationjustice.org

Greenfaith:
https://greenfaith.org

Interfaith Power & Light:
www.interfaithpowerandlight.org

CNN-Enviro members' favourite Wild Goose books/downloads

A Heart for Creation: Worship Resources and Reflections on the Environment, by Chris Polhill

Cherish the Earth: Reflections on a Living Planet, by Mary Low

Enjoy the Earth Gently (PDF download), Ruth Burgess (Ed.)

Field with a View: Science and Faith in a Time of Climate Change, by Katharine M. Preston

Love for the Future: A Journey, by David Osborne

More books and downloads on care for creation from Wild Goose Publications:

www.ionabooks.com/product-category/books/care-for-creation

CNN-Enviro members' favourite websites

About food:

Food Ethics Council:
www.foodethicscouncil.org

Soil Association:
www.soilassociation.org

Climate action for Scotland:

Stop Climate Chaos Scotland:
www.stopclimatechaos.scot

Examples of local effort:

Brighton and Hove Organic Gardening Group:
https://bhorganicgardeninggroup.org
(Talks, allotment experience, etc.)

The Brighton & Hove Food Partnership:
https://bhfood.org.uk
('Non-profit organisation helping people learn to cook, eat a healthy diet, grow their own food and waste less food')

The local Green Party:
www.brightonhovegreens.org

Faith groups reducing their carbon footprint:

Footsteps: Faiths for a Low Carbon Future:
https://footstepsbcf.org.uk

From the USA:

Catholic Climate Covenant:
https://catholicclimatecovenant.org
(For inspiration and resources)

Center for Religion and Environment:
https://new.sewanee.edu/cre
(Annual and local events in the American South)

EarthBeat: Stories of climate crisis, faith and action:
www.ncronline.org/earthbeat

Greenfaith:
https://greenfaith.org
(For ecumenical and interfaith dialogue)

Interfaith Power & Light:
www.interfaithpowerandlight.org
(Country-wide, with many state chapters as well)

Yale Climate Connections:
https://yaleclimateconnections.org
(Excellent science-based newsletter)

Guiding churches through climate crisis:

Climate Emergency Toolkit:
www.climateemergencytoolkit.com

Largest global environmental organisation:

350.org:
https://350.org

Laudato Si':

Encyclical Letter from Pope Francis on care for our common home:
www.vatican.va/content/francesco/en/encyclicals/documents/papa-
francesco_20150524_enciclica-laudato-si.html

Laudato Si' Animators:
https://laudatosianimators.org

Reconciling God, Creation and Humanity:
www.ecologicalexamen.org
(An Ecological Examen from the Jesuits based on *Laudato Si'*)

Protecting wild places:

The John Muir Trust:
www.johnmuirtrust.org
('A conservation charity dedicated to the experience, protection and repair
of wild places')

Woods and wildlife:

Carymoor Environmental Trust:
https://www.carymoor.org.uk
(Educational resources)

Woodland Trust:
www.woodlandtrust.org.uk